CZECH
AND
MATE

CZECH
AND
MATE

FRED AUSTIN

ISIS
LARGE PRINT
Oxford

First published in Great Britain 2009
by
History into Print
an imprint of Brewin Books Ltd.

Published in Large Print 2010 by ISIS Publishing Ltd.,
7 Centremead, Osney Mead, Oxford OX2 0ES
by arrangement with
Brewin Book Ltd.

British Library Cataloguing in Publication Data
Austin, Fred.
    Czech and mate. - - (Reminiscence)
    1. Austin, Fred.
    2. Austin, Margaret.
    3. Czechs - - England - - Dudley - - Biography.
    4. School principals - - England - - Dudley - -
    Biography.
    5. Holocaust, Jewish (1939–1945) - -
    Czechoslovakia - - Personal narratives.
    6. Dudley (England) - - Biography.
    7. Large type books.
    I. Title II. Series
    942.4'93082'092–dc22

ISBN 978–0–7531–9562–8 (hb)
ISBN 978–0–7531–9563–5 (pb)

Printed and bound in Great Britain by
T. J. International Ltd., Padstow, Cornwall

My book is dedicated to the memory of my mother, whose forethought and selflessness ensured that I had a life. Had it not been for her sending me away, I would have been gassed in Treblinka on September 5th, 1942 together with her and my two sisters.

Contents

CHAPTER
ONE

Prologue

I suppose that I had always (in my youthful inexperience!) been attracted by the smaller, darker-haired girls: they fitted better when you danced. Not surprising, therefore, that my eye was taken by the girl in the queue who looked to be no more than 5ft tall, with shoulder-length, dark hair falling onto the simple, blue frock, fastened by its full-length zip.

I forget which of my new friends from "Netherclose" were walking along the queue with me: probably "Hoppy" Hopkins and "Abie" Abram, both of whom were sharing my room at that newly-converted Hall of Residence. In that group of 18-year-olds, I am certain that the dress, with its long zip, will have given rise to a suggestive remark to show that I noticed and it would have been a good topic of conversation as we stood in line waiting to see the Dean.

This was October, 1947 and there had been a good number of changes from the time, 12 months earlier, when I had first come up to Leicester. Numbers had increased from 250 to 450 students, the College had invested in three large and very pleasant houses in Oadby to form the nucleus of the Men's Halls, while

College Hall, based on the former Attenborough house with an added two-storey block of study-bedrooms, had been expanded and re-modelled for the women. Wardens had been appointed and were beginning to shape their little communities to fit their own concept of what residential student life should be.

When I had arrived in Leicester the year before, I had been allocated student lodgings at St. Paul's Vicarage, along with three other men. The rooms were unspectacular, but satisfactory, as also was the food laid on by the Vicar's housekeeper. Curiously enough, one of my fellow-lodgers came from Halesowen, and another from Walsall, places I was quite unfamiliar with, but that I would get to know well in later life when the Black Country became our home. What stands out in my mind about the arrangement for "approved lodgings" is the agreed rent of £2-10 shillings, which turned out to be exactly the same as my income at Taylor, Taylor and Hobson's, where I would soon be working when my grant was withdrawn at Christmas. At College, in the meantime, I had been accepted into the Honours group by Mrs. Patterson, even though my Higher School Certificate results had been deservedly weak. I think that I held my own with the group, which was more than half made up of returning ex-servicemen, a number of whom were married, some with children. The work was not, I think, comparable with the Honours course when Prof. Sykes took control in the following year, so, once again, I was allowed to amble along quite happily.

It must have been that the administrators knew as little about the Teacher Training grants as I did, which is how I came to be supported for a whole term before they and I discovered that the Ministry would not fund me until I had obtained British nationality. The result was that I was in debt to the College for an amount that was never specified to me and never again mentioned: also, of course, I needed help to discover a way of living through the remainder of that academic year. Enter Professor Tibble, whose remit, in addition to the training year for graduate teachers-to-be, included the supervision of those coming through on Teacher Training grants: curious though it may seem, there was never once any suggestion from him of my abandoning the course and I don't think I have recognised sufficiently his good will and his support at what could have been a disastrous turning-point in my life. He it was who found me the job as engraver at Taylor, Taylor & Hobson's lens factory (later, a part of the J. Arthur Rank film empire), where, as mentioned a moment ago, I earned exactly £2-10 shillings a week. No question, therefore, of my staying on at St. Paul's Vicarage: I made a fast move to Wharf Street in central Leicester, where one of my new colleagues, recently married and with a wife who was heavily pregnant, was happy to offer me lodgings at the more manageable rent of £1-5 shillings.

My experience of the world of work on a noisy factory shop floor was enhanced by an almost immediate, enforced holiday, when the icy-cold spell at the beginning of 1947 meant that there was no electricity to run the machines and the factory closed down. However, the thaw that followed allowed a return to a more normal pattern and, for a few months, I lived the life of a factory machinist. If I were to say that I used my spare time in the evenings and at weekends to improve my knowledge of French or English literature, I would be deluding myself and you: I continued with my carefree and generally irresponsible approach to life, waiting for events to happen.

We shall hear a great deal more about Philip Austin, my self-appointed "guardian", at a later stage in this account, but he re-entered my life in June of that year by asking me to come to Burley-in-Wharfedale, where he was organising (together with the owner) a little, private Preparatory School. Being in close proximity to Philip was no longer a great worry, since I felt confident about keeping him at bay. He needed someone to plug a gap in the teaching of Mathematics for the last three weeks of the summer term: as I would be fed and housed and paid something on top, this was an offer not to be refused. It turned out to be an encouragement for a prospective teacher, for not only did I feel comfortable in the situation, enjoying the company of the children and finding the maths, at that level, not too demanding, but the children and the staff seemed to find me likeable. A little glimpse of the Yorkshire Dales was also a considerable improvement over Wharf Street in Leicester!

The year ended with the usual few weeks at Aintree with Philip Austin's mother, followed by a spell at a student harvest camp in Rutland, where physical work on a farm brought in a little extra pocket money in preparation for the return to College. A similar effort the year before had taken me potato picking in the East Riding, making me an experienced harvester for later years in Lincolnshire. And so it was that, when I returned to Leicester to resume my course, I was no longer quite the same overgrown schoolboy who had left Hastings after the 6th Form: the variety of experience had undoubtedly brought, if not a greater maturity, then greater self-assurance, unwarranted though it may have been, to the young man who walked along the line of students in the upper corridor and saw the little girl in the zipped frock for the first time.

CHAPTER TWO

The Story Begins in Ostrava

If, at 18, as a student beginner in Leicester, Fred Austin was, as described in the prologue, immature, irresponsible and irreverent, we must look for an explanation in his earlier life, which differed somewhat from the usual pattern of children brought up in a cohesive family unit. That, at least, was the case after his arrival in England at the age of 10.

Before April, 1939, Fred Austin did not exist and we are now looking at Fredi Stiller, born on December 1st, 1928, into a contented middle-class family in the town of Ostrava (Mährisch Ostrau), a large and fairly grimy, coal-mining town in the north of Moravia, astride the Silesian coalfield which was shared between Germany, Poland and Czechoslovakia. I say "contented", because that is how it appeared to me as I grew up with my mother and sisters, though I have no real way of assessing my mother's feelings when my father died of kidney failure only four months after I was born. It was when we were in Israel and able to ask questions of his brother (my cousin Fredi's father) that we discovered that he had earlier lost one of his kidneys, thus becoming much more vulnerable to the heart attack of which he then died prematurely at the age of 48. The photographs in my Czech album show him as a 30-year-old, in the Austro-Hungarian army and leave us in no doubt as to why my mother, a much younger and very beautiful woman, would have been captivated by his appearance. One of the few things that I have been told about my father is of an incident which took place in London, where, because he loved ballroom dancing, he spent an enjoyable evening, during the course of which his partner fell and, in the process, ruined her stockings. As a gallant gentleman should, my father not only helped her up, but took her name and address and, at the earliest opportunity, sent her a pair of replacement stockings.

At the time of his death, it must have been a very difficult adjustment for my mother, since she would still have been in her early 30s and for Ilse and Trude, my 7- and 4-year-old sisters, but I cannot remember any conversations that would have thrown light on their feelings at that time. It was not until much later in life that I would be told by the same Uncle Adolf in Israel of our family connections with Nowy Targ, of my father's earlier failed marriage, of the first wife who "betrayed" him with a fellow officer and the daughter whom I never knew because she was taken away to Lwow by her mother.

My own mother had trained as a photographer, studying in Budapest for a while and, when she returned to Poland after the end of the first world war, met and married Hynek/Ignatz, that handsome officer. How they then came to settle in Moravia when the Austro-Hungarian empire was broken up is another part of family history which has never been explained to me.

"Contented", therefore, is how it remains in my memory of childhood in Ostrava, with my mother running the family business, selling all kinds of household linens and haberdashery, but perhaps concentrating on handmade men's shirts, as seen in the elegant shop windows of our earlier shop on the corner of the square onto which we looked from our 3rd floor flat. Quite often, as a little boy, I would be taken behind the curtains at the far end of the shop, where the fitting room was, presumably for measuring gentlemen for their shirts, but also used for coffee making and for hiding little boys when customers had to be dealt with! I said "earlier shop" because, at some stage in the later 30s, the business was moved onto the main Masaryk Platz, where the frontage was much narrower, but the actual serving area inside was pretty well the same. The advantage, I imagine, was its location, facing the large open market and being right in the centre of the bustling commercial life of Ostrava, whereas the first shop, though only 100 yards away from Masaryk Platz, on the corner of a relatively quiet, residential street and equally quiet square, would not attract the passing trade.

Looking back now at those first 10 years, I feel very ashamed about how little I really remember of our family life at that time. As well as the shop move, we had, at some stage, perhaps a little earlier, moved flats to a neighbouring building on the other side of Bank Strasse which is still there today. We were now on the 1st, rather than the 3rd floor of a more modern building, which must have been quite a relief when it came to climbing the stairs. Once you entered the flat, it opened onto a long, quite wide and brightly lit hallway/corridor, with a good-size window looking down onto the little inner courtyard on the right. Next on the right was the kitchen, which also had a window down onto the yard. On the left were several doors until, after passing the kitchen, we came to the two rooms that I was most familiar with and which are clearest in my mind: turning to the left at the end of the hallway, the family living room, on the corner of the building, with windows giving onto Bank Strasse in the front and onto the smaller, narrower street on the right, which led me past the synagogue and across the main road to my school. I can visualise the large, round table at which we sat for our meals and which served as my, and probably my sisters', working area for whatever was to be done: I can't be sure about homework, but it is quite possible that I did have some. That same room also had two beds in it: mine on the right and the one on the left for the occasional family visitor. I suppose that there were curtains on the two windows, but I cannot remember anything about them. As was normal then on the continent, there were no easy chairs or settees in the living area but, going back one door along the hallway, there was an elegant "parlour" which I went into only when I was having violin lessons in the last 12 months or so before leaving. Here, with photographs on it, was a grand piano which Ilse, and perhaps Trude also, practised on and which was also used by my violin teacher, who came to the house. This same grand piano was later packed and sent off to England as part of my "trousseau" and will be referred to later. The floor of this "music room" was a highly polished parquet, partially covered by an oriental carpet; there was a chaise longue and, no doubt, other comfortable chairs, but nothing that has stayed clear in my memory.

Going back to the end of the corridor, the door on the right led to my mother's bedroom, where there was a large double bed and a sofa of some kind across the bottom of it. It was a spacious room with, leading back towards the kitchen, a door into the bathroom and, on through the bathroom into the kitchen. Being totally internal, the bathroom always seemed cramped and full of steam, probably because extractor fans had not yet been thought of. As far as I remember, there was a huge gas geyser over the bath and there was always plenty of hot water for my bath on bath nights.

Opposite the kitchen door, on the other side of the hallway, was the other totally enclosed "little room" and that didn't have an extractor fan either. Nor can I remember anything about the decor of these areas, except that it all seemed to be shiny paint and what I would later have described as rather institutional. Even more worrying is my inability to recall ever having seen my sisters' bedroom, which must have been in the space between the front door and the "parlour", on the left as one entered the flat. Maybe it was forbidden territory for boys? Neither can I remember ever getting into arguments with my sisters, which seems a strange way of going on: what family do we know where brother and sisters never argue? In fact, the clearest memory that has stayed in my mind, where all three of us were together, must have taken place shortly before I came away, towards Easter in 1939. By tradition, we used to paint eggs or eggshells with all kinds of bright designs and, while I was doing this, Ilse and Trude were making papier-mâché ashtrays or dishes, which they painted and on which, when dry, they wrote "I LOVE YOU" in the middle. Although, by this time, I must have started my three-week intensive English course, I am certain that my English was not yet up to understanding those words and I had to ask them what it meant, which gave rise to great hilarity.

It was in March, 1939, also that I woke up one night and heard the sound of loud, marching boots in the street below. When I looked out of my bedroom window, I was looking down on a column of German soldiers tramping along Bank Strasse, presumably towards some barracks in the town. That was the night when Czechoslovakia fell. A few days later, I was in the shop with my mother when a German soldier walked in, did a smart "Heil Hitler" towards my mother, then bought a pair of gloves to send home to his wife. I remember that we were both impressed by how polite he was.

My mother being fully occupied running the business and, with continental shop hours being what

11

they were (and still are), there must have been arrangements to cover the hours that we were not in school. Furthermore, since I attended a Jewish school, I can only suppose that Saturdays were a non-school day and that, while I was younger, we had a live-in mother's help, whose job it was not only to look after the children, but also to cook and do the housework. My cousin Annie from Nizna was certainly involved in this, as borne out by some of the holiday snaps in my album, but there must have been others until such time as Ilse was old enough to accept responsibility — and even then, she can hardly have been expected to shop for and feed the family. So, that remains a mystery and, given my later interest in food and cookery, rather a surprise that I recall so little about it!

I do remember, however, that, on Sunday mornings, we used to call in at the patisserie round the corner for some mouth-watering coffee-walnut pastries, which followed the well remembered Wiener Schnitzel that was standard Sunday lunch: there must have been other dishes from time to time, but I cannot remember what they were. Perhaps we did not expect hot meals every evening when mother came home? I remember her cutting large, oval slices from the dark rye loaf which she held against her middle — this, rather than a breadboard, is the way I saw bread being sliced. Then there would be some Liptauer cheese (paprika and carraway mixed in, of course!) and maybe some gherkins. Goulash is well remembered, too, but not any particular occasion when it would be served. Other than that, my outstanding food memory is of being served carp, a delicious river fish, which we never had at home, but when we were invited to join with the Tesarz family for non-Jewish celebrations, probably at Christmas. Chicken soup with matzo-balls I associate with the family gatherings at the Muller household in Witkowitz and that used to take place once or twice a year, at Channuka maybe, or the Jewish New Year, when we went out there on the tram, past the huge iron and steel works, belching out smoke and flames.

The Mullers were a large family that included Cilka and Hella, whom we all remember so fondly, as well as Joe and Robert, who all ended up in Montreal. Father Muller had a cork factory in the town, producing all kinds of products, not only bottle stoppers. But the great attraction about the factory was that it had a window at the back which, if I stood on the lavatory seat, overlooked the skating rink and allowed a free viewing of the ice-hockey matches that were regularly played there. Football, I was reminded by Bela (a family friend from Ostrava) in Israel, I also watched occasionally in the stadium on the other side of the river, where the Ostrava football team had its home.

The two sports in which I actually participated on a regular basis were ice-skating, to which I remember being taken by my sisters and where I did seem to manage to stay upright, and, more regularly, since it was available all the year round, gymnastics, for which I attended the Makkabi Club in the school gymnasium, which I remember to have been very well equipped. This must have taken place after school and gave me the opportunity to gain one or two certificates for proficiency.

The school itself was not a large building, grey and two-storied, and the classrooms were not very different from those in the old Five Ways building in Birmingham, with a long blackboard facing the class and a raised dais at the front for the teacher's desk. All of the teachers that I remember were men, but I may be being misled in that by the class photographs that I have been given. Certainly, my class teacher and the Head were male, the latter being a tall, imposing figure with wavy, brown hair, who always wore a grey, striped suit. I also remember the very strict, older man who taught us classical Hebrew, well enough for me to be able to read the scriptures in the synagogue when called upon to do so — though I only remember one occasion when I was actually standing in front of the congregation.

The classes were large, nearer forty than thirty, and mixed, of course. It is perhaps significant that I remember the girls far better than the boys: this may be because that is where the stronger opposition lay when it came to judging who had the most "jednickys" (a "one" was the best result you could get) on their report at the end of the year or term. Of course, there might have been other, less academic reasons: it was Helga Himmler who was the main competition, as well as the girl who had long ago taken my fancy. The others, like Anita Silberbusch, Bianca Goldman, Ewa Nettel and Ruti Herbach were also-rans, though Ruti, who lived just round the corner from us, over the family

14

delicatessen shop, was a girl with whom I often went to play — doctors and nurses, if I remember correctly, because she had a younger brother who could be "persuaded" to be the patient!

Pavel Bacharach is the only boy that I remember well: the son of a doctor, living not very far away, he used to call for me on his way to school in the morning and we would make our way there together. Being in pairs made it easier to withstand the occasional unpleasantness when our paths crossed with non-Jewish boys going to their own school. On such occasions, there might be some name-calling or even the odd bit of stone-throwing, showing that anti-semitism flourished even in modern Czechoslovakia, though not nearly to the same extent as it appeared to be in Poland, judging by what we learned later.

CHAPTER
THREE

Slovakia in the Holidays

Summer holidays were long and hot, both the length and the temperature being very much on the normal lines of what was to be expected in Central Europe. As happens even today in France, my mother would, I assume, close the shop for a month in July/August and take a well-deserved break with the children in a spa or a riverside resort, where we would have rooms in a "pension". Very few people had cars, so holidays involved a train journey with a taxi at each end, and days spent by the river or going for long walks: the Czech photograph album that came with me has ample evidence of those activities.

As school holidays extended well beyond my mother's time allowance, she would have to make provision for me to be looked after: I remember way back into my pre-school days, being hosted by my uncle and aunt Heimann in Slovakia, where I spent many summer months "going native" with the local farming population (I no longer dare call them peasants, because of the pejorative connotations the word carries today).

Nizna, as the village was called, followed the line of its river with its single main street, lined with its long, single-storey log houses, which are so typical of rural Slovakia, Poland and other rural areas in Eastern Europe. At the southern end, the large single-span bridge took the road across to the other side of the Orava river, which it then followed on towards Podbiel, a larger village, where the station had a goods siding, and there was also the area Police Station, to which Cousin Maria and I walked one summer's day when she was over from the United States. Just this side of the bridge was the "halt", where the "motorka" (single-carriage train) stopped and dropped off the post for the village, meeting which would be almost a daily ritual.

At the northern end, Uncle Heimann had his house. Because it served three different purposes, the house had distinctive features which all inter-connected. In the middle was a long room with long, rough wooden tables and benches, where the locals would sit and drink their foaming Slovak beer out of tankards with lids on (to keep the flies off?) — no bottles in those days. At the far end was the all-purpose shop, which sold not only foodstuffs, but every other need that the locals were likely to come up with: huge sacks of sugar and salt, huge barrels of gherkins and shelves, laden with everything that you can think of, bearing in mind that we were in the 30s. No electricity, of course, so candles and paraffin for the storm lanterns played a large part in what was kept. Tobacco was coarse and was rolled by the men in ordinary brown paper as and

17

when required, not at all like the much finer blends known in England and the USA.

For the living quarters, you had to go to the other end of the building, where the large kitchen backed onto the tavern area, allowing domestic work to be carried on when no attention was needed in the hostelry. All the rooms had floors with wide wooden boards, except the kitchen, where there was a solid stone floor, a large cast-iron oven built into the wall, with a baker's oven beside it, into which the huge, round loaves would be fed on long wooden shovels. Some of the local women would bring their bread or joints of meat to be baked in the oven. No lounge or dining room that I can recall and the bedrooms were simple and uncluttered. All the walls and ceilings were whitewashed and probably washed over pretty frequently, because they always seemed very white. The outside paintwork was the usual rural yellow that is still one of the basic colours for buildings in Central and Eastern Europe, and each front entrance had six or seven steps leading up to it, the extra height presumably serving the double function of keeping the water out whenever the river broke its banks in the spring and also making sure that animals and pests had a separating space.

From the kitchen, there were steps down into the yard, quite a large one, where the chicken and the geese ranged free and, running parallel with the main building, there was a long, equally high hay barn, at the front of which, under the same roof, were four cubicles. The rustic carved doors opened onto a bench seat which, when you removed the round, wooden lid in the middle, had a bottom-sized hole cut out of it and there you sat. A look through the hole revealed the considerable dung heap several metres down below, to which you added your little contribution and which, at times in the year which I did not personally witness, would, no doubt, be carted away by one of the villagers to be spread as fertilizer on the fields. The hayloft did indeed store lots of straw which had that wonderful, clean smell which I can clearly remember. The chicken coop, on the left as you came out of the kitchen, was regularly cleaned out and, while the old straw and contents were added to the dung heap, the clean would be spread around for the hens to live on and lay their eggs in.

At the other end of the yard, on the right, was a tall, wide pair of gates, wide enough to permit the oxen and cart to enter occasionally and bring a fresh load of straw for the hayloft. If you stepped out of those gates, you were then on one of the very few side roads that I remember and, if you went about 50 yards to the left, you approached the blacksmith's forge with its huge anvil and the ever-present flames for heating up the horseshoes. The clanking of the hammer on metal was a constant background music if you lived in its vicinity.

Going further, beyond the blacksmith's shop and now beginning to climb the hillside, with the hill forming the backdrop to the village, you came immediately upon the village church, with its tall, white tower and its bells which rang out morning, noon and night. On Sundays, the villagers and their children, dressed in their colourful best, would process up to the church, past our house, then turning up the side road where the smithy was, having first come along the main street, gathering numbers as each house gave up its little contribution of people.

The village street, going back to the bridge at the southern end, had two obtuse-angled bends roughly following the much smoother bend in the river. Just before the road reached the bridge, it crossed the single-track railway by the little station which became a hive of activity at the two or three times a day in each direction that the motorka passed through. Its distinctive and easily recognisable whistle could be heard for miles as it came up the valley, the noise bouncing off the sheer cliffs on the west side, before the valley opened out into the clearing where Nizna stood. Not only did people come to meet those who were expected, while others went off themselves towards the north or the south, but there would also be those who were loading crates of live chickens or geese for the market or hoping to pick up deliveries from further afield.

The motorka, although it was a single carriage railcar, more like a tram than a train, had a good size freight section for luggage and sacks of post, the latter being removed to be sorted out by the village postmistress, whose combined house and office was back just beyond the first bend in the road.

When we went back to Slovakia in 1963 and visited Nizna, it was just by the Post Office that we met the then komissar, who introduced himself as Johnny Reguli, with a strongly American accent, and who had known the Heimann family and was able to tell us what had happened to the Jews living in the village when they were deported, as were the majority of Jews in Europe.

There was, as I remember it, one other Jewish shopkeeper, called Herzog, whose business was also a general grocery, about 150 yards back from my uncle's at the second bend in the road. How they divided up the village trade I do not know, but I well remember being in his shop and, much more exciting, sitting on his knee in the driving seat of his car, being allowed to steer down the village street, while he, of course, did the necessary on the pedals. That was definitely my earliest experience of driving a car and I was very pleased with myself at this accomplishment. I cannot remember ever having met a Mrs. Herzog and it could well be that there was no such person — indeed, that might account for his being able to afford a car! Mr. Herzog's face is very clear in my memory because he looked so very like my class teacher in Years 4 & 5: he wore glasses, had a roundish face and, behind the glasses, a friendly smile for little boys. His shop was another place where I could expect to dip into the barrel for a gherkin or be given a toffee, just as I might, but it was never overdone, at the Heimanns or, back in Ostrava, at the delicatessen shop kept by Grandma Sterngast, or even at the Herbach shop when I went to play with Ruti.

By the time that I knew him, Papa Heimann was a very old man (probably in his mid-seventies, but looking rather older), always with a flat cap on his head, always puffing on the long, curved pipe which old men smoked in those days, and generally sporting grey stubble on his cheeks and his chin, but never allowing it to develop into a full-scale beard. I have an idea that his skin was too delicate to permit a shave every day and I seem to recall the old cut-throat razor being sharpened on a leather strap, probably by Ali — Annie's husband in the later 30s — who would perform the operation for him.

Grandma Heimann, on the other hand, was slim enough to be called bony and always wore black, though the black was generally relieved by a white apron. Her hair was pulled straight back into a bun at the back of her head, while her face had a beak-like nose and sharp features. She was always busy in the kitchen or the yard or the garden, collecting eggs, gathering raspberries with my help or pulling kohlrabi and carrots for the pot. I don't know if anyone helped her with the garden, but it was beautifully neat and well-organised — no flowers that I can remember, except sunflowers grown for seeds, and certainly no lawn, but all dug over for plenty of produce. She was kind and talked a lot, in contrast to her husband who scarcely opened his mouth except to blow out his occasional puffs of smoke.

Their daughter Annie was, of course, the family member most closely in touch with us, having spent some time — maybe a long time? — in Ostrava, helping to look after us children as a "nanny". I have nothing but pleasant memories of her, both in Nizna and in Ostrava, and I imagine that she would be the one who transported me to Slovakia in the holidays. She must have married Ali in the mid-thirties, when they were both mature and either could not or would not have children, but they were both very good with and to me — I always looked forward to going to Nizna for my holidays and enjoyed my time there.

How we communicated linguistically I have no real idea because, although I spoke Czech and German, my impression is that Slovak is sufficiently different from Czech to make things difficult. The Heimanns spoke German and Hungarian, but must also have been fluent in Slovak in order to fit into the community. Ali, I remember, came from Hungary and when Maria Carleton (born Laufer) visited in the summer of 1938, she certainly spoke Hungarian with them and German with me.

Whatever the answer to that might be, I was, nevertheless, able to play with the village children and to go out harvesting with the villagers, who seemed quite prepared to take me with them into the fields, riding out in their empty ox carts and returning later in the same carts laden high with the harvested corn or the remaining straw from the threshing machine, which was destined for their barns. Whether I actually did anything productive in the fields or simply chased around the stooks of corn and then had a ride back high up on the load in order to roll off into the hayloft, that I cannot remember. However, being with the neighbouring locals, dressed in their rough corduroy trousers, held up by braces, with their coarse linen shirts and topped with wide-brimmed hats to keep off the sun, that I remember very vividly.

They did not have watches, of course, so that our time out in the fields was governed by the sun, which almost always shone brightly, and by the church bells which rang out for vespers. There must have been times, nevertheless, when we had stormy weather, since one of my earliest memories was being allowed to sit and splash happily in the ditch that ran along the front of the house at the edge of the road, after the storm had filled it with water and the sun then turned it all into a mudbath. Those ditches, about 3ft wide and 2ft deep, would invariably be dry in the summer, but were absolutely essential in the winter and spring to provide escape routes for the rain and melted snow which came down from the hillside. They were crossed at each house or yard entrance by stone or log "bridges", wide enough to allow the ox carts across wherever that was needed.

The rail journey to Nizna required one change of train at Zilina, where the express from Ostrava stopped and allowed the pick-up for the motorka that went winding up the valley through Podbiel and Nizna to the Polish frontier. At what stage I began to do this journey independently, I do not recall, but there is no doubt in my mind that, becoming used to independent rail travel in this way, will have made it very much easier in March, 1939, when the time came to leave the family and set off on my own to Vienna, waving "goodbye" to my mother, as her white handkerchief receded on the station platform in Prague.

24

CHAPTER
FOUR

On My Own

The half-dozen or so people in the compartment of the Prague Vienna express must have felt highly sympathetic to the little boy with the card hanging from his neck, asking them to keep an eye on him until he was picked up in Vienna. They probably also realised what a wrench it must have been for my mother to stand there on the platform and let go of me — something which I do not think fully struck home with me until very much later in life.

It was in January, 1939, I think, that I was first made aware of the arrangement that my mother had come to with her cousin in Vienna, whose 15-year-old son had been due to go to England with an English schoolmaster named Philip Austin in the coming Easter holidays. Sadly for my young cousin, the Nazi edict that no Austrian Jew over the age of 14 would be allowed to leave the country put an end to any hopes of his departure. Thoughtfully, the cousin in Vienna immediately spoke to my mother, offering to substitute me in the arrangement and, although at that time in 1939 the Germans had only annexed the Sudetenland, and claimed that they had, "no further territorial ambitions", it must have been plain to anyone who was not as blinkered as Chamberlain that annexation was not going to stop there. That my mother prepared for my departure from that time forward may seem difficult to believe and lots of listeners to my story have wondered how she could bring herself to reach such a courageous decision. That she was far from alone in her decisiveness and her courage is borne out by the hundreds of youngsters who came to England in a similar, but more organised way, on the "Kindertransport".

It was a few weeks later, in March, 1939 that I woke up one night and heard the sound of loud, marching boots in the street below. When I looked out of my bedroom, as mentioned earlier, I was looking down on a column of German soldiers tramping along Bank Strasse, presumably towards some barracks in the town. That was the night when Czechoslovakia fell.

When the time came for departure and before I set off for Vienna and England towards the end of March (Easter must have been quite early that year), my mother and I, on our own, spent a few days in Prague preparing for my departure. There are two distinct memories which have stayed with me of our time there: one is the grey flannel suit with short trousers which she bought me and I then wore for my onward travel. The other is of numerous visits to the Gestapo offices, where we stood in front of stern-looking officers who questioned my mother, before noisily stamping our documents with the German eagle. How many of such officials we had to persuade I cannot recall, but it seemed an endless process. At the end of it all, I obviously possessed all the documentation which would allow me to pass into Austria, Germany and Belgium on my long, circuitous journey to England.

The days and weeks which led up to my leaving Ostrava on this journey, however, are a complete blank. When did I say goodbye to my sisters? What happened when I knew that I was leaving my school for the last time? My relatives and those around me clearly knew that I was about to go — you only need to look at the dedication ("Keep smiling!") at the front of the photo album which I brought away with me and which gives such a clear pictorial history of my first ten years, to grasp that fact. My cousin, Gisela Sterngast, who compiled the album and wrote the dedication, was obviously moved to do this with my mother's involvement, since that is where most of the photos must have come from. But I do not remember any goodbyes, nor anybody seeing us off at the railway station in Ostrava, just my mother on the platform in Prague. Were all of these deliberately suppressed and erased from my mind? I just don't know.

Once in Vienna, I was, of course, met on the station platform by the cousin, whose name I can, unfortunately, not remember and, a day or two later, along came this rather portly, youngish man — Philip Austin always looked somewhat older than his chronological age — just 26 at that time, wearing his favourite mid-brown Harris tweed suit with plus-four trousers. He was tall, thickly built, with an egg-shaped head already well on its way to being bald on its pate, and thick, horn-rimmed glasses to correct his short-sightedness: glasses that he often removed in order to give them a rub and, when he did, revealed rather bulging eyes. Although this description does not sound particularly prepossessing, I do not remember any feelings of dislike at that stage, because he was kind to me and treated me gently, and because there was so much new happening around me that my mind is much more likely to have been on those distractions.

Two days passed, during which much business must have been transacted between our cousin and the newly arrived Englishman to whom I was to be entrusted. Soon, though, my new "protector" and I were off again on the long train journey to Brussels, travelling overnight in a second-class compartment, which we had to ourselves. In those days, third class had wooden benches and would have been likely to be crowded, whereas these seats were padded and had the white, lacy antimacassars that put them in a higher category.

We crossed the frontier at Aix-la-Chapelle, sometime in the dark of the night, woken by the frontier guards, who examined passports and luggage on both sides of the border and put their stamp on our documents, mine being in Philip's possession, as might be expected. As was clear from the nicotine stains on his fingers, Philip was a heavy smoker and, as soon as we were over the frontier, out came his cigarette lighter, but not to light up: instead he removed the cotton-wool wadding and proudly showed me the little collection of diamonds which had been hidden inside — they meant nothing to me, but it was obvious that he felt pleased with himself at the success of his ruse over the customs men. Who gave him the diamonds and what was their source? Another mystery!

In Brussels, we stayed a day or two in a small hotel and had our meals in a cafe that Philip knew well and obviously rather enjoyed. There, he introduced me to such gastronomic delights as fillet steak and chips, and also taught me the phrase — probably one of the only bits of French that he knew well — "*Deux Bass et deux glaces*", though the Bass, I hasten to add, were both for him and not for me! We must have done some sightseeing, because I remember the little statue of the boy urinating and, vaguely also, going to a family where there was a girl of roughly my age, who spoke German and who, if my deductions are well-founded, later married the Earl of Harewood.

And so, over the Channel, another new experience for me, since I had never been anywhere near the sea, followed by my first visit to Liverpool and Aintree, where Philip's mother lived at 6, Caldy Road. The house was undistinguished, set in a row of similar, small, stuccoed villas with three bedrooms, two living rooms, of which the front one was the little-used parlour, and a kitchen that was dark and stretched back to a scullery, coalhouse and inside, but very cold, lavatory. Outside the back door was a little concrete yard and back wall, with an alleyway beyond. I was put into the small third bedroom, where there was a single bed and a small wardrobe — all perfectly acceptable.

Mrs. Austin — whom I must have called "mother", following Philip's example — was a small, plump, rosy-cheeked and cheerful woman, who bustled around the house and gave the impression of being businesslike. This probably stemmed from her nursing training and the fact that she considered herself, certainly at work, to be in a position of some authority over the factory workers to whom she administered first aid. Unlike her delightful sisters Edith and Nell in the Isle of Man, who never put on airs and graces, she had misguided delusions of grandeur and pretensions of being "county", to use her own vocabulary.

I had never come across gas mantles before and I don't think I lived with them anywhere else: the lights were dim and noisy and it comes as no surprise that Mrs. A. was waiting for someone to pay for a conversion to electricity. The surprise was, and she told us this when I was at the student stage, that she was expecting the funding to come from me, once I was in a position to help out of my earnings, since she had never managed to persuade either her husband or Philip to find the money. This lack of electricity was also the reason for my regular missions to the radio dealers where the accumulators for the battery radios were charged up in those days.

I remember her husband only vaguely, having overlapped with him in Liverpool only once, if my memory is correct. He was an engineer on cargo boats and rarely at home, which was probably a good thing, since he and Mrs. A. did nothing but squabble noisily and, in her case, tearfully. He then seemed to disappear off the face of the earth and I was eventually told that his ship had been torpedoed at sea without my ever getting to know him better: neither Mrs. A. nor Philip ever talked about him to me at any length.

For me, the great attraction of Liverpool was its trams, on which I spent a great deal of time riding around and getting to know the different parts of the city, both inner and outer. I now have no idea at all of how I paid for my travel or whether, during the war, children were given a free pass that would take you anywhere. Be that as it may, since Mrs. A. worked as a resident nurse/sister at a large, local factory, I had masses of time when nobody was around and I could occupy myself by either reading library books or criss-crossing Liverpool or going down to the Pier Head and watching the ferries going to and fro from there to Birkenhead, Wallasey and Rockferry. The ocean-going ships were also tied up close by and there would always be something of interest going on.

Any lengthy contact with Liverpool could, however, not have taken place before the summer, whereas, in April, I must have been whisked off to North Yorkshire, where Philip was, at that time, teaching at Ampleforth Junior School and I was deposited with a family in Whitby. Please don't ask me how we managed to communicate when, at that stage, my English must have been absolutely rudimentary. All I can remember of the three weeks that I spent with them is that there were two teenage girls, that the Spinks owned a sweet factory in the town and that I went, very briefly, to a typical 1920s type primary school, in a stone-built building with, inside, those folding partitions which separated one classroom from another, but were able to be opened up to make the hall/gym. The class sizes were large and very similar to the 40s that I was used to back in Ostrava, but I have no clear recollection of how things worked either at school or in the family.

CHAPTER
FIVE

I Make My Bed
With Philip

What is clear is that, within three weeks, my association with Whitby and the Spinks was ended when I was given the choice, which I must have understood somehow, of staying there or going back to Philip, who was leaving Ampleforth and Yorkshire to go to a Preparatory School in Penmaenmawr in North Wales. Why did I choose to go with him when I had no reason to be discontented with Whitby? I have no idea. Perhaps I thought that life with Philip would be more exciting, judging by the time that I had spent with him in those early days after we left Vienna? Or did I misguidedly see a substitute father in him? Whatever the reason, I quickly found myself in a smallish boarding establishment, where I slept in a dormitory with five other boys and was taught in a class of eight. After normal school hours, we did supervised "homework" in a large, airy room and, if we finished before the older boys, we were allowed to play quietly and individually with any toys we happened to possess. The toy I remember most clearly is a little, red Schuco sports car, with a steering wheel which controlled the front wheels and a movable gear stick which actually allowed you to change gear and go into reverse. I must have played with it for hours and, I imagine, it must have been something that I brought with me from home.

How I came to be selected as wicketkeeper for the school team, I have no clear idea, but it happened very early in my time there. The school had an attractive sports field out at the back and we spent a good deal of the summer playing games and practising, which suited me very well. In the classroom, my progress must also have been quite good, since it took me to second (out of the eight!) in the end-of-term exams, by which time I must have been able to read and write English fluently and, having had no contact with Czech and German for four months, was probably well on the way to losing these. All in all, when you add together school, sport, church parades and the closeness of other youngsters, I am certain that the term at Penmaenmawr helped me enormously to adapt and integrate into the English way of life in that warm summer leading up to the beginning of the war.

That term also introduced me to Philip's sexual peculiarities when, on the odd occasion, not yet too frequent, I would be invited to visit his room in out-of-school hours. Can I succeed in thinking myself back into the mind of an innocent and compliant 10-year-old who has put himself freely into the hands of an adult male who, to all intents and purposes, is his sole guardian? Probably not, for I see myself accepting as a necessary and not abnormal part of my life with Philip that I should expect to be kissed and touched by him in a sexual way as reciprocation for his "looking after" me. What was the odd occasion at the boarding school became regular, of course, in Liverpool in neighbouring bedrooms and even more so in Reigate (his next job for the first two or three weeks of the Autumn Term) and Hastings, where we lived in rented rooms for the time that Philip held on to his teaching post there. However hard I try, I do not see myself struggling to get out of his clutches, because the ten-year-old that I was could not be expected to realise that this behaviour, never before encountered, was anything other than normal and to be incorporated into his "new" life, even though it was contrary to his natural inclinations. At what stage he progressed further, I do not recall. This, I can safely say, was neither to my liking nor, by then, thought of as something to be accepted with equanimity.

Was there a way out? Of course not. Quite apart from the youngster's lack of understanding of the situation compared with the more worldly-wise of today's television generation, to whom could he have turned for advice? There were no other adults in his life to whom to talk and, in any case, he had every reason to be loyal to this man whom his mother expected him to trust. I am positive that, at that stage in 1939/40, even after hostilities began, there was no idea in his head about the fate that was in store for his mother and all the Jews left behind, so that it would not be true to say that there was an element of gratitude for having been spared their future fate: that could only be much later. But the sort of loyalty one feels to one's parents must have been there and, in spite of all that took place, remained there until he was considerably older.

By this time, the reader will have realised that Philip was an exceedingly mobile young man, having moved from Yorkshire to North Wales, then to Reigate, quickly followed by Hastings, all in the space of six months. It was only later that I came to understand two highly relevant factors which led to Philip's short-lived hold on these teaching posts — 1. he was extremely accident-prone in the laboratories where he was allowed to teach Chemistry, but his tenure would end when there was an explosion, and 2. the reason behind 1. was that he was totally unqualified to teach Chemistry or anything else. True, he sported a graduate gown and a fine, white ermine, Cambridge hood, but he had no right to them and had, in fact, left school at 14. He was a self-made cheat and charlatan, with the result that accidents occurred frequently in his laboratory.

While Philip lasted out at Hastings, a number of things happened which, though trivial, have stayed impressed on my mind: we occupied two rooms in a house overlooking the town from the side of one of the several valleys which run down towards the sea. Though not too far from the school, it was far enough for me to be granted a bicycle as my daily transport and this, I thought, was a great step forward in my development. Our rooms, on the first floor of a typical

Hastings house — not unlike the one that I came back to when I lived with the Croucher family after the war and quite similar also to the house in Cleethorpes where Margaret's family lived — had the usual small open fireplace that bedrooms used to have and there we sat with a toasting fork, making large slices of toast, liberally buttered and spread with jam, as our bachelor tea. Because of Philip's involvement on the staff and my having missed the normal time for the 11+ examination, I was given a special internal exam even though I was not yet 11, which allowed me to be placed in 2J, the top group in the first year, with whom I then spent the next four years and with whom I was very happy.

The teaching staff at Hastings were also a very friendly group, meeting socially in their staff room one evening a week. As a newcomer on his own, Philip was allowed to take me along and I watched them playing cards and chess and used to be allowed into their store cupboard cum tuckshop, when invited by someone who wished to offer me a treat. At all events, Philip must have become sufficiently friendly with Mr. Lawrence, a young member of the staff, recently married, to ask him to take me on as a lodger when Philip's next disaster struck in the Junior Chemistry lab and he was, once again, given the push. The Lawrences were very kind and soon incorporated me into the family, which included a terrier puppy, who took us for long walks after tea and gave me a playful, but very sharp, bite in the palm of my hand.

CHAPTER SIX

The War and Evacuation

This pleasant, but brief, interlude ended at Christmas, when the whole school was evacuated, as a body, to the supposedly safer location of St. Albans. Hastings was, of course, obviously in the front line should an attack ever come, but St. Albans, so close to London, was certainly not clear of all danger from the bombs that followed: nevertheless, it proved to be a safe enough place to sit out the war from January, 1940 until the summer of 1944. Philip, in the meantime, had gained promotion to the joint Headship of Barnfield School, a small private enterprise on the hill in Kent where Bromley, Hayes and Beckenham meet. This was obviously a more satisfactory arrangement for him than trying to teach Chemistry, for he actually managed to stay at Barnfield for several years during the war and, for me, it became as frequent a holiday home as Liverpool.

Being at Barnfield brought me into much closer contact with the war, for we were then at the height of the Battle of Britain and close to Biggin Hill aerodrome, a prime target, over which there were frequent dogfights to be observed. The hill on which the school building stood, though it was undoubtedly in the midst of residential housing rather than any kind of industry, often came in for what might be termed residual or secondary bombing from planes which had not found their way to, or had been prevented from reaching their primary target area. The worst of these incidents occurred one night when, having decided that we would risk staying in the house, rather than going out into the cold night to the air-raid shelter which offered little comfort, a number of land mines came down in our area. One of these can have been no more than 50 yards from the building, on the school field. Quite apart from the terrifying noise of the explosions and the shaking of the school building, we were covered in falling plaster and masonry, though, when viewed in the morning light none of the damage turned out to be quite as serious as we had thought. What was even more comforting was the relief when we saw the shelter, a long brick and concrete structure, intended to provide safety for the schoolchildren whenever there was a daytime air raid. It was completely wrecked, with its concrete roof having collapsed into the brickwork: had we been sheltering there, we would certainly not have come out of it alive.

It was also at Barnfield (and I must have been about 14 at that time) that an incident took place — I think it must have been in the Christmas holidays — which has remained very clear in my mind. I was persuaded, in return for the promise of a £5 note, to drink a whole tumbler of brandy, the idea being, I assume, that the drink would make me more amenable to Philip's sexual needs. Whether I succeeded in downing the whole glassful I am not sure, but I must have drunk a sufficient quantity for it to result in my passing out for a considerable length of time and throwing a fit which, as I only understood later, could have had very serious consequences. Fortunately, it did not, but it obviously worried Philip greatly for he not only brought in the doctor immediately, but also restrained himself from ever trying that approach again. There was a lasting consequence, however, in that, for many years, until well into my married life, I shuddered at the mere thought of alcoholic drinks. I think also that this incident marked a change in Philip's approach to me, in that I was much less troubled by his sexual attentions from that point on. I put this down to the fact that I was getting older, perhaps more independent, and perhaps, as a result, becoming less attractive to the paedophile in him — pure speculation! It would be nice to think that, perhaps, the incident shocked him into a realisation that he was responsible for this teenager's welfare: but that, too, is purely speculative.

Back in term-time St. Albans, my very first night of evacuation was one to be remembered: whereas everybody else had arrived in a special train from Hastings, I arrived a day later from Liverpool and defeated the organisation of those good people whose task it was to place us all in billets. I, therefore, found myself taken for an overnight stay at the workhouse and spent the evening sitting round the table with a group of men who, though very obviously down-and-out and reliant on the charity of the corporation, were extremely kind to this youngster who had been thrust into their midst. Their dormitory was large and filled with beds at 6ft intervals and the night was noisy with coughing and men going back and forth to the rather smelly toilets. However, the next day I was removed to the home of a genteel, grey-haired lady, who had obviously been left in a financially sound and secure position by her dead husband, who had been a clergyman in Ireland.

Mrs. Rice had an attractive four-bedroomed house, brick-built in the twenties or thirties, in a quiet, tree-lined cul-de-sac, just a short walk from the town centre and not too far either from the buildings which Hastings Grammar School had been allocated as its temporary headquarters. All four bedrooms in Mrs. Rice's house were now occupied, since there was a paid companion, Miss Whitty, Mrs. Rice herself, both ladies in their late 60s, as well as a paid housekeeper, who changed from time to time.

The result of all this gentility was that I rarely set foot in the kitchen, that meals were served at a regular hour, appearing through the hatch from the kitchen into the dining room, and that, in spite of whatever rationing was applied during those war years, I was well and properly fed — "properly" in the sense that there was no sloppiness and that good manners were always insisted on. St. Albans had a good market on Wednesdays and Saturdays, and the two ladies and the housekeeper obviously knew where to shop for good results, because my memories are of nourishing meals, well served. Furthermore, at lunchtime during the week, we were able to go to the Community Canteen, for which we were given tickets at the beginning of the week, when the school meals register was taken. The meals there were also very edible for an omnivorous child, though I remember puddings which we described as "chocolate concrete!" All of this, plus the daily bottle of milk and the hot bread at morning break from the bakery just down the road, meant that we never went hungry.

Living in a cul-de-sac before there was much car traffic meant that children were safe and the road was a good play area where I had friends to play with. The house had a calm front garden with a large horse chestnut tree, whereas the back was green and open and very well looked after — by a gardener, of course. I was allowed the dining room for homework, which was not always my first priority, but was certainly encouraged and, once that was done, I could read my library books in the sitting room, on a little stool usually, sharing in the coal fire and listening to whatever was on the radio. Since the ladies enjoyed good drama and good music, this became part of my regular diet and, no doubt, had quite an influence on my later tastes.

At weekends, I would often join with class friends in longish walks, where we seemed to natter about anything and everything, but that, of course, was in addition to the organised football and cricket, for which we had the use of a field out on the road to Harpenden.

Games were on Wednesday afternoons as well as Saturdays, when there were normal lessons in the morning, and were much enjoyed by most of us: even though I was no skilled footballer, I seemed always to end up keeping goal for whatever age group I happened to be in. Cricket was rather better, not only because of my wicket-keeping prowess, which dated back to the Prep School in North Wales, but also because I developed sufficient determination to stay in and held my bat straight, making me a reasonably solid opening bat. In the earlier years, I also kept the score book for the first eleven who, at that stage, seemed like grown men to me and I enjoyed the travelling with them to other schools around Hertfordshire and the status it gave me, in that I knew many of the prefects in that context.

Two other activities helped to occupy my leisure time fruitfully: I must have joined the Scouts very early on after my arrival in St. Albans. We were extremely fortunate in having a school troop, with two of the masters completely devoted to its organisation. We met in a hall just up the hill from Mrs. Rice's house and not only learned to master the tying of knots and the maintenance of our bicycles, but also played all kinds of competitive games to round off our meetings. At the beginning of the summer holidays, there would always be the summer camp which, I think, lasted a fortnight and was, for me, a thoroughly enjoyable experience. It taught us the basic skills of cooking over a campfire, orienteering and finding our way through the thickest of woods, the mixed pleasures of living at close quarters

43

in a bell tent with other boys of differing ages, gathering
with them around a huge campfire in the evenings and
benefiting from the open-air life. In winter, we had the
rehearsals for the scout pantomime, in which I
graduated from the young chorus to the solo female
and, eventually, to the magician, once my voice had
broken and depending on whether it happened to be
Ali Baba or *Jack and the Beanstalk* that was being put
on. On Sundays, we were expected to report for the
church parade at St. Peter's and the thought of gaining
exemption on the grounds of being Jewish never
occurred to me: why should it? Never once since
leaving the family had religion been mentioned and I
simply joined in with everyone around me. St. Peter's
was not very high church and there was no pressure to
take communion or to do any other than turn up for
the roll-call and join in with the hymn singing,
something which I have always enjoyed. At a later stage,
like many of my contemporaries, I joined the Youth
Club attached to the church: this is where I first
became more seriously interested in table tennis,
snooker and, most importantly, the local Grammar
School girls, who came to the club in goodly numbers.

Being evacuated resulted, of course, not only in the
personal displacement of each pupil and each member
of the teaching staff who, presumably, found rented
accommodation around the town, but also in the
corporate displacement of the school as a functioning
institution. The organisation was in the hands of our
rarely visible Headmaster, Mr. Hyder, who had
negotiated the buildings of the Spicer Street Methodist

chapel, with its attached little hall and school rooms, where all the morning classes were held, to be followed on most afternoons by the more specialised Science and Art classes in the St. Albans Grammar School buildings, just down the road towards the Cathedral. A greater contrast can hardly be envisaged than that between the very good laboratory provision in the afternoons and the dingy, rough classrooms in our Spicer Street building. At morning break, we were simply turned out onto the street, which was a good excuse for going round the corner to the bakery for some hot bread rolls or even a small tin loaf! The marvel, however, is that, rough and ready though it was, it must have worked adequately and we, the boys, continued to feel part of the HGS body ending up with reasonable examination results in the School Certificate, which I sat in 1944, just before we returned to Hastings, once the Normandy invasion had taken some of the pressure off the South Coast.

An additional and quite interesting aspect of the school organisation and layout was the location of the Headmaster's office in the Abbey Gateway, standing between the Grammar School and the Cathedral, at the top of the narrow road leading down to the Roman remains at Verulamium. This must have given Mr. Hyder a very sheltered, if not totally isolated, existence from the normal bustle of school life: indeed, I cannot recall seeing him around the place at all, apart from the assemblies, which were held in the body of the chapel itself, with its ground floor pews supplemented by the large, semi-circular gallery, to which we graduated as we moved up through the age groups. Even when we returned to our own premises in Hastings (Guliemus Parker fundavit in 1568!), where he had his office by the main entrance, as one would expect, Mr. Hyder did not seem to venture greatly into the deeper reaches of the school and I cannot recall his ever having taught me anything in the classroom, or even stepped in as a substitute for an absent member of staff. Reverting to the Abbey Gateway, however, the Head's study on the first floor, at the top of an ancient stone staircase, was shared by his secretary, a lean man in his thirties, by the name of Ferguson, who must have been excused his military service, since he had a gammy leg and always walked with a stick. In the normal run of events, I would probably never have seen the inside of the Head's study, but the said Mr. Ferguson was a lover of classical music and had built up a considerable library of records: add to this the radiogram which was placed in the Head's study and you have the makings of a Classical Music Society, which used to meet on Sunday afternoons in the winter. How I became involved in these meetings and who persuaded me to go, I have no idea, but I soon became a regular attender. So, these afternoons of Beethoven, Schubert, Mozart and Tchaikovsky, when added to the radio at Mrs. Rice's, most certainly awoke my interest in serious music and prepared the way for the concerts at the White Rock Pavilion in Hastings which came later.

After three happy years with Mrs. Rice and her ladies, I was moved (for reasons which were never made absolutely clear) to Mr. and Mrs. Broome, a very inoffensive, retired couple who lived in Beaumont Avenue, a good deal further out of the town centre, making me much more reliant on my bicycle for everyday transport. They were nice, quiet people who left me largely to my own devices and put me under no pressure concerning my school work, which suited me well. They offered me one advantage, however, in that they themselves spent most evenings on home assembly of electrical parts which, when put together, formed some kind of switch-gear for a local factory — payment by completed piece. The Broomes were perfectly content that I should join in with this assembly work and encouraged me to earn a little extra pocket money in this way, thus supplementing the irregular weekly amounts which arrived from Philip. One other unexpected bonus came to me with this move to the Broomes — Derek Croucher, a boy in my class with whom I had previously not had much to do, lived close by and we used to cycle together on our way to and from school. Thus, when, in the summer of 1944, the return to Hastings came on the horizon, it was perfectly natural for me to talk to him about the problem which I foresaw, namely, that I would have nowhere to live when the school moved back to Hastings and I came down to start in the Sixth Form. Derek, good-natured soul that he was, offered to ask his mother whether she would put up with me as an extra body in the family and solve my problem.

CHAPTER SEVEN

Sixth Form Back in Hastings

So it was that I packed my bags once again and, without either Philip or I having to do much in the way of arranging, I was accepted into the Croucher household on Derek's recommendation and, for my part, I simply became one of the four Croucher boys, which I was very content to be. Since Mr. Croucher was only home intermittently, his butchery skills having been called up into the RAF, Mrs. Croucher was the one who steered the family through the war years and did it very competently: all of us, as far as I remember, co-operated with her without any rebelliousness and carried out whatever tasks were expected of us. Colin, who was only ten when I arrived, was about to start his secondary schooling and, like Derek, was bright enough to have a Grammar School place. Brian, aged 14, was totally different and about to leave school to work in the shop which, in Mr. Croucher's absence, was run by two or three of the ladies in the family, backed up by an older, former butcher, who did the heavy work. Brian was delighted, I remember, when he was old enough to start riding his father's motorcycle with its box side-car for delivering customers' weekend meat and for going back and forth to the family allotment which he organised on the other side of the valley from the shop — on the side where the council estate was built, in which, so I was assured, people kept their coal in the bath!

Derek, who must have been at least a year older than me, even though we were in the same form, was a calm, peace-loving boy, who liked nothing better than sitting at the front-room piano, playing all kinds of popular music, both from sheets and improvising. He was really very accomplished and it annoys me now that I never delved into the history of how, being evacuated to St.Albans like me, he had managed to gain that skill. Derek was also a very respected member of the school's Air Training Corps, in which he had already risen to the rank of sergeant and, before very long, without completing his Sixth Form course, he flew the nest to join the RAF, returning two years later, after completing his National Service, to train as a teacher in primary education. This left me, after several months of sharing the double bed with Derek, in sole possession of the back bedroom, except when Derek came home on leave.

With Mrs. Croucher, you always knew where you stood. She was, at one and the same time, relaxed and friendly with all of us and had an iron fist inside the velvet glove, which we all respected. She fed us well, ran the house efficiently, without making any great song and dance about it, did her part in the shop and also knew how to relax. It was she who got me regularly involved in whist drives, from which I certainly learned a great deal about how to think and marshal my forces in a game of cards.

Both at home and at school, I enjoyed my life at Hastings, tending to tread the line of least resistance as far as work was concerned, being put under very little pressure, compared with what I expected of Sixth Formers when I was sitting on the other side of the teacher's desk. Financial support from Philip was not as regular as it should have been and I remember the occasional moan from Mrs. Croucher about his contribution not arriving when it should. Nevertheless, I seemed to manage to pay for the occasional game of snooker, the odd Saturday night dance at the White Rock Pavilion and, from time to time, a visit to the cinema with whoever was my girlfriend at the time. The White Rock also hosted the occasional concert of classical music but I had discovered a way of climbing up into the false ceiling of its dome by way of an opening at the rear, where the building backed onto the steep cliffside, thus gaining totally free access. These were my first live concerts and I suppose that the view, looking down from overhead at, for example, Moura Lympany playing the Tchaikovsky Piano Concerto could never be equalled when sitting in the stalls or the circle! More normally, my diet of classical music was provided by the radiogram in the middle room, to which I was allowed unrestricted access both for home reading and for the listening which mostly accompanied it. The rest of the family tended to live in the back kitchen, where the fire was, Colin being too young for homework and Brian having no academic pretensions.

In school, the return to our own building in Hastings in September, 1944 opened up new possibilities to those of us who stayed in the small 6th Form of those days. Upper and Lower Sixth had to be taught together, but the syllabuses made allowances for that and, even then, we were only five or six for French, three for Latin and I was on my own for Geography and the subsidiary German which was taken by a visiting clergyman. The teaching staff were, I am sure, very good but, I now think, did not make nearly enough demands upon a student like me who has always been too easily satisfied with a "that will do!" approach. Thus, without any great pressure either at home or at school, I drifted along very contentedly to my mediocre Higher School Certificate in 1946. The Sixth Form had no enclosed room of its own; instead, it was given the gallery overlooking the Assembly Hall which, once morning assembly was over, was only used for the occasional Music lesson. Our "free" periods were, therefore, uninterrupted and not supervised by staff, resulting in considerable progress being made both in our chess and our bridge skills. Where the bridge came from I cannot recall, but it fitted neatly with the whist encouraged by Mrs. Croucher and it carried over nicely to my later life in the Leicester College Hostel, where late night card parties were the rule. My cricket was also much improved by the school's unlimited access to the Hastings Cricket Ground in the centre of town, which was as well maintained as one could wish and had the very best of practice nets — a great improvement over our facilities in St. Albans. Quite apart from the playing area, it offered me the opportunity of being involved with Miss Read, who ran the refreshment kiosk and also provided lunches and teas for the professional sides who participated in the Hastings Cricket Festivals in August and September. I quickly became one of her regular and trusted helpers whenever I was not personally involved on the pitch. Obviously, I spent far too much time around the cricket ground in my various roles but, fortunately for me, by the standards of the time, it did not prevent my being admitted to University College, Leicester where, after a false start, I had to make up for it by spending an extra year on "Intermediate" before going on to Prof. Sykes's Honours course. Being Miss Read's helper also allowed me to supplement my meagre pocket money a little and meant that I did not feel too deprived by not yet having entered the world of work, where most of my contemporaries now were.

Although I still kept a sufficient contact with the school Scout troop to participate in the Christmas pantomime as Abanazar, or some such baritone character, I had, by this time, graduated to the Air Training Corps, where I rose to the dizzy heights of corporal. I think we used to train on two evenings a week but, more interestingly, we, too, had a summer "camp", when we were taken to Lee-on-Solent or some other RAF station to be given some realistic service training, which could include time in the air. On one such memorable occasion, I was taken up in a two-seater Tiger Moth and actually allowed to manoeuvre the plane in the air — a highlight in my air training career! My life on stage also expanded beyond the pantomime because, now that we had the use of a stage of our own in the Assembly Hall, Mr. Wright, the Latin master, would produce a play in the Easter term, giving those interested a chance to shine. Having no girls available would, of course, have placed severe limitations on the plays he could choose: *The Amazing Dr. Clitterhouse* was certainly no masterpiece, but I enjoyed playing "Lefty", a cheeky little crook. This led to my being given the lead part of Tony Lumpkin in the following year's production of *She Stoops to Conquer* and I made my mark with that, even gaining praise in the write-up which followed in the school magazine. When you add to that the occasional participation in choral singing that we used to take to local churches, you can see that my involvement in school and out-of-school activities was considerable and, equally, that the opportunities given to me by the school, even during the war years, were far from limited. I suppose that, up to a point, it also accounts for my less than total devotion to the academic work which might have been expected of me.

The outcome of my schooling at Hastings, therefore, was that I faced the world confidently, because everything had come to me with ease, but with minimum academic qualifications, since my HSC passes were just that: bare passes. What did I want to do as a career? My only suggestion when this question was asked was that I might volunteer for the RAF, having had a good grounding in the school ATC. However, this proposal was never fully tested, since Philip was convinced that I should go to University — nobody at school had pushed me in this direction (or any other!) — and had obtained the necessary application forms from Leicester and from the Ministry of Education, who were, of course, very anxious to promote teacher training. I cannot remember there being any argument from me about the pursuit of this course of action and I certainly owe Philip a debt of gratitude for insisting that I take up his suggestion. Had I gone towards the RAF, I suspect that I might, there also, have come up against the wall of not being a British subject, just as I did at the end of my first term in Leicester. As it was, his insistence proved, in the end, to be both my salvation academically and my personal fulfilment, in finding the girl in the blue zipped dress who was to pull me out of the mire of irresponsibility and lack of motivation. That fateful meeting, to which I pointed at the very beginning of my tale in the Prologue, was still another year ahead, in 1947, after the hesitant start which was a mixture of University, those few months of factory life, school in Yorkshire and holiday weeks in Liverpool, followed by potato picking at harvest camp.

CHAPTER
EIGHT

Leicester,
October 1947

As opposed to my false start in Leicester in the previous academic year and the rather drab accommodation in St Paul's Vicarage, arrival at Netherclose was much more stimulating. We were all "freshers", starting out on something new, both in terms of study and communal life (these were Leicester's first venture into Halls of Residence), the Halls had beautiful grounds which the October sunshine allowed us to enjoy and our wardens, as evidenced by the meeting on the first evening, seemed both pleasant and relaxed. Somebody was soon tinkling on the piano in the Common Room, a little later somebody suggested a group walk into Oadby to taste the beer in the local hostelry and then, of course, a bridge session at the end of the evening, allowing me to use the skills acquired in my 6th Form days. Even the walk up the road to Middlemead for morning and evening meals was a social event in which I became better acquainted with the students who lived in other parts of the Hall, such as the nine "Rochdale boys", all from the same school, who shared the long second floor room which stretched the whole length of the house.

No question of my proceeding straight to Honours French, as I had the previous year: both Professor Sykes and the Dean, Professor Bryan, looking critically at my results in the Higher School Certificate, were quite insistent on my pulling myself up to a decent standard by taking Intermediate in French, German and Latin. I think it began to percolate into my awareness at long last, that I would need to settle to some serious work if I was not to end by being rejected, as some were, by a demanding Head of Department. The work I was doing, however, was well within my capabilities.

Though my ballroom dancing had been picked up in Hastings on a very haphazard basis, which meant that I never really got to grips with the slow foxtrot, I did enjoy it for its own sake, as well as for the opportunities it brought in female contact. Fortunately, therefore, I was at the Palais in Humberstone Gate for two of the Saturday dances before the Freshers' Social, which was the highlight of the first term. On the first Saturday, I only managed one dance with "Zippy", the girl who had caught my attention in the Dean's queue, but I made up for that when the second Saturday came. By this time, I was definitely "hooked" and hopeful, making sure of the last waltz and my place at her side when it came to escorting her home. Strange as it may seem, so firmly was she labelled "Zippy" in my mind, that it did not occur to me, at that stage, to find out her real name and that was something that was deferred until we were walking back to Hall after the Freshers' Social.

However incomplete my previous year in College might have been, it nevertheless had put me in a different category from those who had only just arrived, since I knew a lot of the established students and was known to them. As a result, and unlike the real freshers, I was fully involved in the performance of *Death among the Ruins*, the lively show that was being put on as an entertainment for the student body — it was a clever reworking by Norman Sharpe, an ex-service English student and enthusiast for W. S. Gilbert, of various extracts from Gilbert & Sullivan comic operas, sufficiently memorable to come frequently to mind, even today. Because of my involvement and the help I gave in clearing out clutter from the stage and wings, I did not arrive in the hall until the dancing was well under way and found, to my dismay that a rival for "Zippy's" attention had booked five dances ahead! How dare he? I made sure of dance number six, which, as luck would have it, turned out to be the last waltz. That was good enough for both of us, for Rex (the Villain), in spite of his assiduity, had not made the best of impressions.

It was on the short stroll back to the Women's Hall that it finally occurred to me to ask "Zippy" for her name: "By the way . . . ?" When I heard the name "Thelma", I knew that it would not do. "Have you got another name?" I went on to ask and, to my relief, was told that it was Margaret, a name that I have never tired of, though used only in reference when speaking to third parties, whereas "darling" and "sweetheart" spring much more readily to my lips. In spite of the "generous" extension until the end of the Social that the girls were allowed on that evening, time was still very limited, but it did, at last, permit a proper kiss good night, as opposed to the glancing peck which was all that I had been allowed on the previous Saturday. From then on, from the end of October, 1947, we were inseparable and recognised by our fellow students to be so. We were together for study, together for lunches, together for the relaxed period which followed lunch and for every possible spare moment in the evenings and at weekends. The University library, at that time, was conveniently arranged with cubicles down one side, in which the table with two chairs allowed the two of us to share that semi-privacy and, because Margaret was, by nature, a most conscientious student this was where I acquired her good habits and became the promising young man that Professor Sykes, in his wisdom, recognised.

The previous year's obstacle to my receiving state funding still needed to be overcome and it was not long before my naturalisation papers came through. Thus it was that, in November, Margaret accompanied me to the office of the Commissioner for Oaths who was specified to hear me swear my allegiance to King and Country. No more danger of having my grant withdrawn and, what is more, I was now entitled to apply for a British passport, not an immediate necessity but soon to be one when it came to being sent to France for my study year abroad. By this time,

Margaret was familiar with my history and had been shown the album that contains all the family photographs that I brought with me from Ostrava. This privileged viewing — I cannot remember any occasion when I had shown it to anybody else — took place at Netherclose, where I had invited Margaret to be served with beans on toast for tea, my equivalent for introducing her to the family! Looking back at the 18-year-old that I was then, I am amazed both by my having the album with me and by being able to produce it when the occasion demanded, for I was not the most orderly or organised teenager and yet, I obviously looked after this treasure with great care, as I have done until today. However, if you were to ask me where the album was for the first eight years of my life in England, I would not be able to give you any definite information.

In the short space of time before my birthday on December 1st that year, Margaret had made up her mind to present me with a hand-knitted, Fair Isle pullover. Imagine my surprise and pleasure, bearing in mind the very few items of clothing that I possessed, at being given such a gift, hot off the knitting needles and ready to wear through the rest of that winter. Imagine further the skill and devotion of the knitter who, in a matter of three weeks, keeping the whole venture a secret from me, had managed to deal with a complicated pattern involving four different coloured wools, most of the time in bed after "lights out", in the dormitory that she shared with three or four other girls in the former Attenborough house. If I had not realised it before, I certainly began to understand then what a treasure I had become involved with.

Soon, it was time once again to earn some money at the Post Office, where the extra deliveries at Christmas gave ample opportunity to supplement my income before going back to Liverpool for the remaining time before term began. I managed to sort out a fountain pen for Margaret, and a tin of American biscuits, preserved from a parcel that Aunt Paula sent, was my Christmas present to her family, who I had heard a great deal about but not yet met.

Just after Christmas, while still in Liverpool, and by a strange coincidence, since I was destined to spend no more holidays there, a very distinguished-looking gentleman came to the house to interview me about Philip. He had the look and the bearing of an ex-officer and he had his questions well prepared in a notebook, in which he wrote detailed answers. The questions were mainly about my relationship with Philip and, though I do not have a clear memory of the detail, it is not difficult to piece together this detective work with what we found to be the case later: namely, that the authorities had finally caught up with him and a prison sentence would follow.

Although, at that stage, nothing was either said or done which ended my association with Liverpool, things were happening at Cleethorpes about which I knew nothing at the time, but was soon to be informed. Inevitably, Margaret discussed our association with her mother and put her in the picture concerning my history, including the full story of my relationship with

Philip, just as I had made it known to her. Mrs. Colam, as I then thought of her, was full of indignation and immediately insisted to Margaret that I was not to go to Liverpool again and certainly not to have any further close contact with Philip. "He's to come here!" And that is exactly what I did from Easter 1948 onwards, but I did keep in contact, both with Mrs. Austin and with Edith and Nell in the Isle of Man, where Margaret and I had a memorable holiday the summer before I went to France.

CHAPTER NINE

I Become a Colam

Giving up Liverpool for Cleethorpes was no great hardship and exchanging Mrs. Austin for the Colam family even less so. I was made to feel at home there by everyone and had no difficulty in settling in, since they all, from the two-year-old Raymond upwards, accepted me with ease. Remarkably also, the layout of the house in Harrington Street was absolutely identical to the Crouchers' house in Godwin Road, Hastings, apart from having another floor with two bedrooms superimposed. These were the sleeping quarters of the Appleyard family: Clarice (Margaret's older sister), Mark, her husband, Byron and Kenneth, aged 12 and 10 and, finally, Raymond, whom I have already mentioned, toddling between the two households, since he was everybody's favourite at that stage.

There was never any doubt about who was in charge in the Colam household: it was Mum. She had a routine that worked like clockwork, with every day having its duties laid out and adhered to and mealtimes nicely slotted in to fit. She and Clarice worked together very happily (or so it seemed to me) on the cooking and shopping and Mark made an important contribution by bringing home his fish allowance, which enabled fish to be a regular and frequent menu item. I am sure that I was well used to fish and chips before I went to Cleethorpes but, equally, I am quite certain that any previous fish and chips did not measure up to the fresh Grimsby variety that I was now being served.

Margaret's younger sister, Mavis, had left school at the then leaving age of 14 and was well established as an alteration hand at Guy & Smith's, *the* department store in Grimsby, where she was a young apprentice in a large section attached to the Ladies' Outfitting department. Mavis breezed in at lunchtime and in the evening, expecting the meal to be ready and waiting, which it invariably was, and shared her day's events with the rest of us, generally having something hilarious to tell us about Peggy Hall's father, or some disaster that had struck the workroom or, possibly, the outrageous demands of one of the ladies who needed their outfits altered. We were all rather taken aback when she told us about the customer who came to the fitting room to have her new purchase altered and proved to be stark naked when she removed her fur coat! Although she was nearly three years younger, Mavis felt distinctly more adult than Margaret because of having a wage, even though it may not have been more than a few shillings at that time. She, too, had a steady boyfriend, with whom she went out either dancing or to the cinema quite frequently, though it was not too long before Swanee was called up to do his

National Service in the army. Margaret's father, a skilled fitter, was, at that time, working as a Chief Engineer on trawlers and would be away at sea for 10 days or so at a stretch. As a result, he was not there for a few days after my first arrival in Cleethorpes and his return was something which, I imagine, caused me some little apprehension, since I had been told that I was classified by him as a "cruel continental", who was likely to treat his womenfolk as "chattel". Although this pronouncement had been ridiculed by Margaret, who reminded him of how he treated his own wife, it must have been a matter of some interest to see how he would react to meeting this "cruel continental" in the flesh. In the event, Pop, as Raymond called him, and I were soon on the easiest of terms and he very quickly confided in me concerning his mathematical studies, with which he was involved, from time to time, on a home-study basis.

Largely because of my needs, since my income from Philip Austin was now very hit and miss, Margaret and I both took the opportunity of working during the holidays in various capacities: the most immediate was as filing clerks at the local Income Tax office in Grimsby, where we eventually established a little "niche" for ourselves to which we returned time and again. From the previous year, I had already become accustomed to finding a week or two of postal work, either sorting or delivering, especially at Christmas time, thus adding a little supplementary income to my normal allowance, which allowed me to think in terms of modest Christmas presents: the fountain pen for

Margaret and the tin of American biscuits for the Colam family. No comparison, of course, to the pullover which I had received for my birthday and which I have already described.

In the summer of 1947, before going back to Leicester, I had done some weeks at a student harvest camp in Oakham, Rutland, (in 1946, it had been potato picking in Yorkshire) and it, therefore, followed quite naturally that we should book ourselves in to work on the land at the beginning of our summer holidays. We were allocated to Butt's Green, outside Chelmsford, where we were housed in army bell tents and were transported to various farms for harvesting barley, wheat and flax under a broiling sun which resulted in many a sorely burned back where the shirt came away from the trousers (or skirt). The work was demanding and not very highly paid — about seven pence an hour in today's currency — but the camaraderie was good and we had some amusing adventures, like seeing Margaret chasing the farmer's father round the field on the tractor when she did not know how to stop the machine; or hearing from Blagojevitch, the Yugoslav prisoner of war, who had witnessed it, about Chris, the foreman, dealing with a fieldmouse up his trouser leg. However, the main intention behind earning this extra income was to enable us then to go to London with our little pile and spree it on visits to the theatre, afternoon and evening where possible. We went in the cheapest possible seats, of course, and enjoyed an eclectic mix of productions, ranging from *Annie Get your Gun* and *Oklahoma* to *The School for Scandal* which starred

Laurence Olivier and Vivien Leigh. It may only have been three days, but we crammed in the maximum possible, adding an extra day by taking the overnight train to the East Coast. We broke our journey in Boston (at about 6a.m.) and I was duly taken along to meet Margaret's grandmother, various aunts, uncles and their families and especially Harold and Florence, who died so recently. In the short space of a few hours, I met both the Coxes and the Colams and began to feel that I had gathered a large family, in addition to the Cleethorpes branch, which had already stretched to include the sea-going brother Stan, Norah, his wife, and their three children. Our stay at Butts Green was not without incident, for Margaret, who was not greatly accustomed to the outdoor life, took time to get used to its demands, especially as she was housed in her tent with a strange couple, one of whom was a very masculine and powerfully-built lady, whereas her companion was a frail young woman, who appeared to be totally dominated by her motorcycle driver of a friend. Because we were together, however, everything was bearable, even when the newly-arrived cooks, straight from their Domestic Science training course, served up a rabbit pie, cooked only for the time that it took to bake the pastry lids! I should have said "almost bearable", because the effect on Margaret's digestive system (and she was not alone!) was definitely violent.

Spending holiday weeks in Cleethorpes allowed us, over the years, not only to return frequently to the Income Tax office for additional income, but also for me (since I was always the one who was in need of topping up my meagre and irregular allowance) to find more lucrative employment in a great variety of fields where casual work, especially in the summer months, was available. Thus, I gained experience in a wide selection of agricultural jobs in the Lincolnshire countryside, including the back-breaking loading of two cwt sacks of corn of Nickerson's Seeds, from which I returned covered in tiny harvest bugs which burrowed under the skin and were the very devil to overcome. Rather later, when we were already married, it could be labouring on building sites with men who opened up their lunch time sandwiches and threw the contents on the brazier ("bloody ham again!"), so that they could toast their bread, while I looked on enviously over my cheese and beetroot. Once I had passed my driving test in 1951, at the third attempt, having forfeited my second test by arriving a day late, it opened up new possibilities for me, like driving ice-cream vans all over the Leicestershire countryside, playing pretty tunes to attract the population out of their houses, or delivering lemonade by lorry to the seaside restaurants and bars near the seafront at Cleethorpes.

On one memorable occasion, perhaps in my third year of going to Cleethorpes, Stan, Margaret's brother, who was then a mate (in other words a first officer) on his trawler, offered to take me along on their ten-day trip into the North Sea as "trimmer below", which meant that I had to spend my time in the coal hold, making sure that the coal reached the opening from which the engineers shovelled it into the boilers. As a job, this became harder the longer we were at sea since, while the hold is fairly full, the coal simply needs a helping hand to tumble down but, in the later stages of the trip, the movement of the coal is more and more dependent on vigorous shovelling to bring it to the place it needs to be. Add to this the storm and high seas on the 4th, 5th and 6th days at sea, which meant that the hatches had to be tightly fastened, and it will be understood that the temperature inside the coal hold was raised to such an extent as to cause inordinate sweating and difficulty in breathing. I also learned a great deal on that voyage about the way in which a tightly-knit group of men become interdependent. For my part, I don't think I have ever eaten with such an appetite, partly, no doubt, due to the energy I was expending, partly because I was attempting for the first, but not for the last time to give up smoking, and probably also because the food on board — freshly baked bread and fish fresh out of the sea, eaten at all sorts of times of the day including for breakfast — was as appetising as any that I have been served before or since. So great was my consumption of food that the skipper was heard to complain to Stan that I was eating all of their likely profit from the trip — the three officers on the trawler (skipper, mate and engineer) made their money on a percentage of the final profit, rather than on a fixed wage like the rest of the crew. I actually came away with £20 after the ten-day trip which, for me at that time, was a considerable fortune, bearing in mind that I had also been very well fed. My other unseen profit was a heavy load of coal dust on my scalp, which stayed with me until such time as

Margaret was able to give me several energetic scrubs once I was back in Harrington Street.

In the meantime, having completed that first year of Intermediate studies, followed by a happy summer of agriculture and being together at harvest camp, then in the family at Cleethorpes, I felt thoroughly integrated into the Colam household and life as a separate entity was just unimaginable. As soon as we returned to Leicester, Margaret joining her London friend Win in very undesirable "approved lodgings" in Welford Road, I went back to Netherclose, only to find that the University had changed the set-up and we were no longer left to live life as freely as had been the case in the previous year. Bishop had arrived! What it was exactly that drove me into immediate revolt I cannot now remember, but there was a full-scale meeting of all the students in the three houses that were now linked under the wardenship of Richard Bishop and it was instantly clear to me that I would not live happily under his regime. I handed in my notice immediately but, of course, there was no getting away from the "contract" which stipulated that a full term's notice was required, meaning that, since the Christmas term had been broken into, I would have to stay and lump it until Easter. We also had a new Bursar/Housekeeper, whose ideas on the food to be served to students did not meet with universal approval. I am sure that not all the meals were as open to criticism as the one that I particularly remember — tripe which, though cooked in milk, was seen as specially revolting by most of us: we simply refused to touch it, whereupon the Bursar, a dour

Scottish lady, determined to assert herself and show who was in charge, served it up again the next evening — only for it to be ignored again. The fish and chip shop in Oadby did well that night! There was another factor which, no doubt, also influenced me in my disillusionment with Hall: my dormitory friends, Abie and Hoppy, had not returned after their first year, their results being too disappointing. However, we kept in touch with Abie who, eventually, was to be my Best Man and who was a perfect gentleman in looking after Margaret when she passed through London on her way to Brittany at Christmas in 1949, when I was over there for my year as English language assistant. The outcome, however, on the residential front, was that I moved into lodgings for one term at the end of Year 1 Honours, after which, as will be related shortly, I would be spending a year in St. Brieuc. The digs in Highfield Road had one great advantage: they were only a short walk from Margaret and Win's second effort at lodgings, with Mrs. Jeffreys, about which I am sure that she will have something to say in her writing!

With a much sounder language base, my Honours course was now progressing well and, as a student in a good group of four men and nine women, I was holding my own without any great problem. The effect of my association with Margaret had been a remarkable transformation in my ability, or should I say willingness, to concentrate on my studies and to produce work of a standard which brought me to the approving attention of Prof. Sykes who, in his way, was prepared to take me under his wing. Being aware of my financial shortfall on the Teacher Training Grant, which had only two more years to run, whereas I needed three to complete the Honours course and then my Dip. Ed., he quietly arranged for me to apply to work as an "assistant" in a French school one year earlier than my contemporaries, thus buying time to sort out my shortfall during my year's absence. He did also suggest that I might be wise not to be so deeply involved in my "romantic entanglement", but that was simply evidence of his not being aware of how much I owed to this same entanglement.

When June came round, with Margaret's 20th birthday and my now fully-arranged departure for the year in France in the offing, we took the firm step of making our engagement official by choosing and buying the ring from the jewellers in Granby Street, where we had so often stopped to admire the trays in the windows. Margaret, by that time, knew without hesitation the exact ring that she liked and that I was able to afford, thanks to the waiter's job that I had been doing at the Evington Working Men's Club, on the outskirts of Leicester. The three-stone sapphire and diamond ring was a very fitting symbol of our involvement and confidence in each other which, I am sure, made it easier to face the prospect of a year's separation.

And so it was that my first year Honours course was rounded off with a very creditable result and we went off to the now regular harvest camp for six weeks or so, with my picking strawberries all day, while Margaret, who had started off by also picking fruit, was soon called upon to go into the kitchen as assistant cook, when the girl who had been appointed to the post walked out in a flare-up. Not only did this new position give her a steady wage of £3 instead of being dependent on piecework and the vagaries of the weather, but I think she found being in the primitive kitchen a preferable task. This time there was no spreeing of our earnings on London theatres, but a realisation of the fact that our future togetherness would increasingly be based on having some savings to fall back on. Furthermore, the experience of those few weeks in the kitchen gave Margaret the confidence to apply for the post of Head Cook the following summer, when we went once again to the same camp at Leverington near Wisbech. We filled the remaining weeks of that vacation in part by taking up Edith and Nell's kind offer to stay with them in the Isle of Man and then, up to my departure for France, we enjoyed the home comforts of 70, Harrington Street, where we were always well looked after.

CHAPTER
TEN

France, Here I Come!

Armed with my recently acquired British passport and a suitcase which easily contained my entire wardrobe, I said a tearful farewell to Margaret on Leicester station, having helped her first to the "new" flat that she and Win had reserved in Clarendon Park Road. Our academic year of separation had begun and there were no phones that we could afford to use other than in emergencies. We fully expected to be entirely reliant on the post for contact and made to each other the firm promise that we would write every day, though not necessarily put the letter in the post every day. This was a promise that we both kept, even though for me, poor correspondent that I had always been, it was an amazing feat of love and loyalty.

The crossing from Southampton to St. Malo was, even in those days, an overnight one, with curtained-off bunks in the lounge, deep down in the ship's bowels. It was the following morning, therefore, that I found myself on the train to Rennes, where I changed to the express for St. Brieuc. That was the moment when I first realised, and it came as quite a shock, that I was not up to understanding a conversation between the natives when I was not actively involved and when no allowances were made. It will seem strange to the young of later generations that, largely because of the war, but also because of financial limitations, we were not used to foreign travel, except when the war imposed it as a necessity. In Margaret's case, the ice had been broken by the visit of her school pen friend, Daniel, who came from Paris to spend the '46 Christmas holiday at her house — and they are still friends today! — but, for the boys of Hastings Grammar School, there had been no trips or school parties abroad.

My arrival at the Ecole Normale de Garcons in St. Brieuc was totally without fanfares and with very little recognition by the staff, who expected me to settle in without their help, without any introduction to the pupils, with no guidance concerning the materials to be used or the goals to be aimed at. It was very much a voyage of discovery as far as my classes were concerned, though I could rely on the friendly assistance of the two resident "surveillants", Rene and Jean, who knew their way around most things. I think it was the Econome (School Bursar) who showed me to my room and made me aware of the financial facts of life: my (princely) income of about £30 a month, from which my food and lodging would be deducted, leaving me with about £22. From this, I would soon be paying my monthly railcard to Rennes and the enrolment fee on the University course there. Coming from the English University system, where everything was made manageable by the grants provided, I was pleasantly surprised by the French pattern which, without any grant being necessary, was within easy reach for tuition costs, provided you were able to find your own way of paying for board, lodging and travel. Thus, I ended up not only enrolling for the Diploma courses in French language and literature which were specifically laid on for foreign students like me (other assistants scattered around the area, or those who came for a few weeks or months simply to learn the language), but I also signed up for a course leading to the degree certificate in French Philology.

All of this was made possible by two facets of my life in France: firstly, that my timetable for teaching 12 hours per week of conversational English was sufficiently flexible to allow all of my groups to be bunched into two and a half days, thus leaving me ample time to attend my courses in Rennes. Secondly, and equally important, "Charlie" Adrien Favre, on the French staff at Leicester, who had become a friend and for whom Margaret and I had often done favours like babysitting, gave me an introduction to his younger brother's little family, who happened to live in Rennes (marvellous coincidence!), who were amazingly kind to me, in that they not only allocated a bedroom for my use when I stayed over for lectures on consecutive days, but they also fed me evening and morning and I cannot remember ever contributing.

Very quickly, then, I was into a routine, since there was no time lag between school and University terms in France, where, though I was mainly based in the school in St. Brieuc and accepted fully into that community, I would be missing for two or three days each week in term time to pursue my courses at the University. Easy though this sounds, it involved getting myself up at 5a.m. twice weekly and walking 15 minutes to the station to catch the 6 o'clock express to Rennes, then walking another 30 minutes from the station to the Faculty of Arts building, which was through the town centre and on the other side of town, often through the rain which was as frequent a phenomenon in Brittany as it is in the English winter. All of this travel would have been quite beyond my reach were it not for the monthly railcard which, at that time and still in 1953/4 when it was Margaret's turn to travel, worked on a gradually reducing basis, i.e. the price was cheaper as the months went on, making it affordable even on an assistant's meagre income.

I ought now to explain that the French Ecole Normale is something that we do not know in the English educational system: every "Departement" (County) had one for boys and one for girls, making the transition from basic secondary education to teacher training which, in those days, led unashamedly towards teaching in Primary schools only. Entry was at 16 and the first two years led to the basic Baccalaureat, while the next two extended their general education but in parallel with instilling the necessary skills for the classroom. The boys who started on the course ended as men whom the Departement/County allocated to teaching posts within its boundaries, usually in fairly easy reach of their parental home. It may be understood from the above that, in line with their basic educational attainment from an extended Primary schooling, the boys' knowledge of English was, in most cases, elementary in the extreme, especially when it is also borne in mind that foreign language teaching in 40s France, perhaps even more so than in the England of that time, was heavily based on book learning, with hardly any effort to include the spoken word in the classroom, even though there was an oral examination in the Baccalaureat. For someone totally inexperienced in teaching and of a similar age to his students, therefore, there were considerable challenges in attempting a whole hour of English conversation with groups of boys. Add to that my almost total isolation from the English teaching staff, whom I scarcely got to know during the year and who were quite happy to let me drift along.

Living in the school, though fairly spartan as far as my own room was concerned, had great advantages on the human contact side, since the boys were very happy to see me linked into their activities and the resident staff treated me as one of their own number. Thus, I accompanied the school football team on its coach visits to other schools in the same league, learned to join in with rowdy songs while travelling and also picked up a good deal of material for my classroom discussions, which tended to be as much in French as in English. These excursions also brought home to me the layout of the Brittany countryside which, otherwise, would have remained unvisited. The resident staff, with whom I sat down at meal times on the "top" table (very basic, just like all the other tables) consisted of Rene and Jean, the two surveillants responsible for the supervision of boys in their study time and in their dormitories, who, like me, were University students; M. Rolland, a highly qualified Philosophy teacher who lived in Paris and came down to St. Brieuc for the working week, and M. Leduc, who seemed to be parted from his wife and living a bachelor existence. All of these took me under their wing and made it their business to introduce me to whatever I was unlikely to have come across in my life as an English student. This included not only outlandish food like leaf artichoke, to be eaten by dipping into the vinaigrette and making a pile of detritus to be cleared away, or radish as a starter, dipped in salt and accompanied by lavish bread and butter, but also pointers as to where in St. Brieuc to look for my needs and how to make a good start to my student life at the Faculty in Rennes.

The hard-working chef in the school kitchen became a good friend of mine, allowing me to arrive back late on those evenings when the express from Rennes brought me in at about 8.30p.m., starving at the end of a long day. He would invariably find me a nice piece of steak and something to go with it, which I was privileged to eat in the kitchen while we had a natter about the affairs of the day.

Looking back on it now, it seems extraordinarily strange that I drank no wine during the whole of that year (and for quite a number of years afterwards), since it was always served at the weekend as a special treat, in place of the daily rough cider which accompanied all our meals. The reason for my dislike dates back to the incident, described earlier, when I was bribed to drink a tumbler of brandy, resulting in my throwing a fit — as you can imagine, however, the others at the table were quite happy to dispose of my share.

The spartan room, which I referred to earlier, was next to the medical room to which boys were sent when they were ill and for medical inspections, in a wing of the school which was otherwise deserted. The floors were, of course, left as bare boards and resounded to each footfall. The room was long and narrow at the window end, the ceilings very high, with windows and door narrow and high to match. At the wider door end, there was a primitive wardrobe and a washbasin. That apart, there was a hospital type bed and two radiators, one at each end of the room. Everything was painted a dull sort of grey, exactly like the sanatorium next door and the corridor outside, a door at the end of which led through to the wide staircase, at the foot of which the boys would all leave their clogs when they went up to their dormitories (having kept their slippers on inside!). The huge collection of clogs, all gathered at the foot of the stairs, made quite a strange sight for anyone not familiar with Breton habits, but had the very desirable result that the boys were able to go upstairs in their slippers without scratching the polished floors and also, because these clogs were made of solid wood with metal studs, saved a great deal in shoe repairs. Above their clogs and trousers, both boys and staff tended to wear grey overalls or lab coats, whose purpose was to stop their other clothes being soiled. I cannot now recall what the arrangements were for laundering shirts, underwear, etc., but there must have been some facility to which we could turn, since I did not have to do my own washing nor did I go a whole year without a clean shirt and underpants! I do, however, vividly recall, just down the road towards the town centre, one of those communal wash houses which, at that time, could be found all over France and where the women could still be seen "batting" their washing with the typical wooden boards which they had for the purpose — part of their weekly routine, corresponding to Margaret's mother's Monday washday in her scullery, when she would agitate the washing with a dolly peg in her washtub and then scrubbing it before moving the whites on into her corner boiler.

Having passed the wash house and the street where I turned off twice weekly to go down to the station, it was about 15 minutes down the hill to reach the large marketplace with its attractive theatre/concert hall and impressive post office, before crossing to the main shopping street, with its variety of commercial attractions and patisseries displaying their mouth-watering pastries and cakes. In Rennes, too, on the days when I was there, I became familiar with the town-centre shops and cafes, the even more impressive Municipal Theatre in its central square and the broad boulevard which led down to the huge station building. Where the Favre family lived, on the same side of town as the Faculty of Arts, in a quiet street, they had a small back garden with a substantial tree which my bedroom window almost touched when it was opened and which sheltered large numbers of birds who sang their hearts out in the early morning. Henri Favre worked from home for a firm of advertising consultants and was a first-class artist, having had some of his designs accepted for national poster campaigns. The one I particularly remember was for Perrier water, showing a bottle cap on top of a stick, looking like a colourful umbrella or parasol. His wife, Danielle, was a softly-spoken mother of two young children, who looked forward to my coming as a bit of excitement to liven up their week, while their mother turned out to be another of those several ladies in my life who seemed to enjoy mothering me — and I hope that I showed my appreciation.

The Faculté des Lettres was the usual sort of French educational building of the late 18th or early 19th centuries, probably taken over by Napoleon when he drove out all the religious orders, with a large inner courtyard onto which all the downstairs rooms opened directly. It was in one of these large lecture rooms that I and about 50 or more students listened intently to Mlle Pelletier, a formidable lady in her early 40s, who stood no nonsense whatever the size of her audience. She was unusual, too, as French lecturers go, in that she was absolutely rigorous in setting work for the week that we were out of her sight and equally rigorous in testing it the following Friday when we came back for two more hours of her subject. Norman Branson, also an English "assistant" in Vitré, a similar sort of distance from Rennes, but going towards Paris, and I, being English, must have stood out in Mile Pelletier's awareness of the group, because she would frequently turn to one or other of us for her answers but, since

Norman had already completed his degree at Nottingham and I had done one year of linguistics at Leicester, we were usually able to cope.

At the end of the year we were rewarded with a creditable pass in French Philology which, together with the other, less demanding Diplomas, gave us a half of the Licence-ès-lettres. Not only was this an achievement in the eyes of Prof. Sykes and the other staff at Leicester, who had never known it to be done before by an undergraduate, but it really eased my remaining studies, giving me a tremendous advantage over my fellow students for the last two years of my degree course.

CHAPTER
ELEVEN

Christmas in Paris

All of this time, the promised daily letter between Margaret and me was being written, but not necessarily posted on the same day. At all events, it was something to look forward to and gave added zest to each day, especially when I returned from an overnight stay in Rennes. There was also the promised visit due to take place during the Christmas holidays and shortly after my 21st birthday: we had worked out that her fortnight's stay would allow for a few days in Paris after the week leading up to the school's end of term. Feeding Margaret during that week was easy, for M. l'Econome made no difficulty over linking her into our school meals on payment of the usual charges, which he would deduct from my monthly salary. As for her appearances in the refectory at mealtimes, they not only went down well with the staff, whose table we shared, but caused a minor sensation among the boys, who were not used to having a pretty girl sharing their mealtimes and who made no secret of their admiration.

Since we were coming up to Christmas, Margaret was included in the party atmosphere, which was an experience for both of us, with lots of singing, recitation and general French merriment.

However, there had remained the question of where she was to stay. Fortunately, almost as soon as I had arrived at St. Brieuc for the beginning of the school year, I had found my way to the Church of the "Nouvelle Heloise", a protestant group with a pastor who was English. Though long settled in St. Brieuc, married to a French lady and owner of a coal merchant's in the town, M. Stamp was now in his 70s but still speaking French with an atrocious English accent. I have no recollection of how I discovered the existence of this group, where I was warmly welcomed by pastor, wife and little congregation. As soon as Mr. and Mrs. Stamp heard of Margaret's intention to come and stay, they very kindly offered to put her up in their house and they looked after her like a daughter (Margaret's words!). It was here that Margaret was first introduced to a French breakfast, with bread bought in once a week and then, after the first day, having to be steamed in order to be palatable!

Both Margaret's arrival and departure were at St. Malo, where I was able to reach her by a little diesel railcar which ran along the coast to Dinard, on the other side of the Rance estuary, which then had to be crossed by ferry. This was both more direct and cheaper than the route I had taken through Rennes on first arriving. How I managed to finance our trip to Paris with its two hotel rooms, our meals, concert at the Palais de Chaillot and several theatre visits, all our travel and the incidentals out of my first three months earnings, having also paid for my railcard to Rennes, my University registration fees and my living costs through to the New Year, I just cannot imagine. Life in France must have been very reasonable at that time for we certainly did not feel that we were deprived. True, we always went in the highest gallery at the theatre and that was cheap, we always studied the restaurant menu with great care and chose what was reasonable, and hotel rooms in France have always compared very favourably for price with England, especially in back streets like the one where our little hotel stood. All in all, then, we managed extremely well and had an excellent holiday, which included a meal with Daniel (Margaret's faithful pen friend) and his parents, and another evening with M. Rolland on his home territory, where we and the two surveillants had been invited to meet his wife and enjoy her excellent cooking. It was an evening full of lively incident, helped along by M. Rolland stabbing the joint with a bayonet and by Rene's wonderful English when, after making a mess on the tablecloth, he exclaimed "I have made a festoon of myself!" Looking back, I think we not only made the most of that week but we realised how lucky we were to be in Paris: it really was rather special.

It was in the February of that year in France that I first met my cousin Jack Singer when he came over to Paris on business, probably on his way to Poland to buy some of the products which he imported and sold on, or maybe still representing Dupont nylon. I must, obviously, have kept in touch with him sufficiently for him to know my school address in St. Brieuc and to invite me to come to Paris to meet him. I managed this by taking an overnight train and then making my way to the Hotel Scribe, a very swish place near the Opera, where Jack was staying. Not only was this my first adult meeting with Jack, but my very first face-to-face contact with any member of my family since leaving Ostrava, apart from the dim and distant couple of days with Joe Muller in my first year in England, when he was living in Mornington Crescent, believe it or not, before he was interned in the Isle of Man and later in Canada. Thus, my meeting with Jack was quite a memorable one and he went out of his way to make it so. Knowing from Aunt Paula how much I relied on her clothes parcels, he took me to an outfitters and bought me a new suit which, as far as I remember, was the first brand-new outfit I had had, apart from school blazers and trousers and then the sports jacket and trousers that Margaret and I saved up for in Leicester. It was then that Jack filled me in on the efforts he had made early in the war to get my sister, Ilse, out of Czechoslovakia but, of course, without any success. It was not until later that I found out about his complicated wartime travels from Italy, where he had been studying Civil Engineering, to the Philippines and the horror of the Japanese camps, before being able, at the end of the war, to work his way across to the USA. At all events, it was a very special day together before I travelled back to St. Brieuc on the following night train — two sleepless nights were manageable at my then age of 21, but could not be cheerfully contemplated now.

CHAPTER
TWELVE

Back to Leicester

Very quickly, though, we were back to the routine of exchanging daily letters, Margaret working all hours preparing for her finals and my continuing the twice weekly visits to Rennes, fitted around the conversation classes at the Ecole Normale. Financially, my situation eased after Christmas, as my railcard became cheaper and my savings for the end of the year began to accumulate, though they never amounted to a fortune. Among the many friends made during that year, only one lasted through to later life: Herve, the son of a bank manager in Guingamps, remained a contact for many years, firstly when he came over to do his year as "assistant" in Derby, where he met his wife Misette, who was also doing her year abroad, but then in Germany, where we visited them on our return from Toulouse, and later still in Brittany, when David exchanged with Odile, their daughter. My year in France, resulting as it did in the passing of all my examinations, was most encouraging since it laid an extraordinary foundation for my second and third years back in Leicester. Having gone off to France a year earlier than the rest of my year group, I was now linked into the following year, whom I found it easy after my 10 months in France to outshine, especially as my accent and fluency in spoken French helped me so much. This "new" year group was, however, a much more socially cohesive and friendly lot, making it easier for contact with the staff on those Wednesday afternoons when Prof. Sykes had instituted a lecture for the whole of the department, either by an insider or an outside lecturer, after which we all retired to the refectory and discussed the content informally over our cups of tea, with staff fully involved. The group was also regularly invited to socialise at the Hemmings's, Margaret being allowed to join in. It was this, I think, which led Dr. Hemmings then to branch out, making use of the talent in the group to put on a French play, Anouilh's *Antigone*, in which I greyed my hair to play the part of Creon.

While I was doing my belated second year, Margaret, who had completed her degree course the previous summer, achieving a very creditable second class, was embarking on her education diploma, after considerable indecision concerning the direction to follow in her career. She had never been enthusiastic about teaching, but I think this was largely because she lacked the confidence and did not see herself being able to control a class. The deciding factor, however, which did not allow her seriously to consider training in personnel management with Marks & Spencer or becoming a forewoman in a bakery, was her insistence that she should stay in Leicester for as long as I was still a student there. As it later turned out, the teacher training was a very wise decision in the long term, because teaching at all levels gave her great satisfaction up to and beyond the point of her retirement, as well as some wonderful contacts and relationships with both pupils and staff in the various jobs which she tackled with remarkable success.

By this time, after my return from France, life had also become much better on the home front, for I divided my time between the back bedroom at the Czyrkos' in St. Albans Road and going for my meals to the flat that Margaret shared with Win, where I made my financial contribution to the cost of the housekeeping and we ate rather better than had been the case in approved lodgings. The Czyrkos were a lovely Polish couple, well into their 50s, who had settled in England after the war because of political difficulties, together with the Major's batman and cousin, Maciek, their married daughter and, last but not least, their granddaughter Ewa, who was everybody's delight. They were thrilled with my Czech/Polish origin, my knowledge of a few words of Polish and the fact that I was prepared to learn a few more. In their kitchen, there was always a cup of tea on offer, poured through the tea leaves in a strainer in the Polish way and, on special occasions, a slice of walnut cake, which has become the traditional "Polish" in our family, since Margaret was given the recipe by Mrs. Czyrko.

It was that year that I was supported by the Czech Refugee Trust Fund, who stepped into the breach for the extra year that I had needed for the Intermediate qualification. The credit for having made the arrangement and for having found the source of income goes to my Professor Sykes who, in spite of his fierce and crusty exterior, was always prepared to go the extra mile for me and, probably, for most other students he accepted into his department. As a result, I had a seamless progression through the second and third years of my degree course and, of course, through the Education Diploma which followed. When you add to that the income from the many and varied holiday jobs which I undertook, I was able to scrape along quite well in spite of having, by that time, very little contact with Philip Austin and not expecting any further help from that quarter.

To give a full description of the different holiday jobs which I tried would require a chapter on its own and I have already spoken about the Tax Office, the harvest camps and the lifting of huge bags of corn on and off lorries at Nickerson's. The trawler trip with Stan was a one-off, whereas Christmas postal work was a regular, as was the night portering on Leicester railway station. There were the building sites and, later, the ice-cream and lemonade vans and lorries. Margaret, in the meantime, did a regular Saturday at Woolworths from which she saved up enough to buy a little BSA three-wheeler and, for some little while, I did two or three nights a week in a Working Men's Club, but "resigned" when it became too much of an interference with my work. Nevertheless, I have long been convinced that this variety of experience was not only good for supplementing my meagre income, but it also brought me into contact with a wide variety of people from all sorts of background and made me aware of how others lived and thought. This is why, in later life, I always encouraged young people, including our children, to look for vacation work rather than stay at home twiddling their thumbs.

Years two and three of my degree course, therefore, passed quickly and painlessly, with Margaret first of all doing her teaching practice at Willow Mead Secondary Modern School, followed by four terms at Elbow Lane in central Leicester, when she started her teaching proper. Her experience at Willow Mead, where she worked in conjunction with an older lady and quite enjoyed the "special/backward" group, misled her into taking on a similar group of girls at High Cross (Elbow Lane). It should, even then, have been quite unthinkable for any right-minded Head or Adviser to allow a young probationer to take on 26 girls who were not only mixed in age from 11-14, but were also recognised as having learning and behaviour problems. The only redeeming feature that I can find in her having been subjected to four terms of misery with those girls and an unsympathetic Head is that, as a result of that experience, all her teaching in later years proved easy and, most of it, enjoyable. Certainly, that was the case with the remainder of that second year, when she transferred to a delightful class of infants at Harrison Road Junior, where she really began to flourish. I, in the meantime, achieved the great bonus of a 1st Class Honours degree as part of the best year group that Prof. Sykes had ever had, with four of us achieving 1sts, seven more getting Upper 2nds and the remaining two with Lower 2nds. It would be difficult to overestimate the boost which that result gave to my self-confidence (though some would say that I had never been lacking in that department!) and it was the best possible insurance for our future in the year that we had chosen to get married. I hope that it compensated in some measure for my lack of organisation in my financial affairs, for when it came to paying for the wedding suit which had been made to measure at Knight's in Granby Street, the money just was not there in my Post Office account and, to this day, neither of us has been able to work out just where it went. Fortunately, the wedding rings from Lumber's had been sorted out and paid for, but it was Margaret who, as often in my life, came to my rescue by somehow juggling her savings. My own restricted resources and hers (I think she was left with £27 to her name) were practically eliminated by the rings and the honeymoon and, not for the first time, we were left with very little other than our earning power.

Whereas Margaret, with the help of Mrs. Gisborne, her landlady, had been steadily sewing her wedding dress and other outfits for her trousseau through that finals year of mine, my own time had, understandably, been fully taken up by my studies, which led up to the examinations in May and June. They began with the Orals, which were hardly a worry, then moved on to the eight three-hour exams, for which I was pretty well prepared. I suppose that, nevertheless, the next few weeks up to the second half of July must have been a little nerve-racking, until the envelope was pushed through Margaret's door, with a smiling Mr. Chad over the wall and a note from Prof. Sykes asking her to congratulate me on my First. There could not have been a better wedding present for us and it is easy to imagine Margaret's excitement as she woke me with the news in my little back bedroom in St. Albans Road.

The wedding was scheduled for Saturday, August 2nd and I went on selling ice creams until a couple of days before, then drove to Cleethorpes in our "new" 1932 original Hillman Minx, which was to serve us well for the next three years. The BSA three-wheeler had had its share of ups and downs, more particularly when we undertook the 100+-mile journey up to Liverpool to see Mrs. Austin, having obtained for her a small, black kitten to replace the cat that she had recently lost. To round off the tale of the BSA three-wheeler, it was on the outskirts of Liverpool but, fortunately, on a direct tram route to Aintree, where Mrs. A's house was, that it decided to run completely out of oil (which it had been consuming at a fairly alarming rate) causing the engine to seize up. In those days (1952), the solution was to have the cylinders rebored and to fit oversize pistons — not too expensive, since it was only a two-cylinder engine *but*, it has just occurred to me, perhaps swallowing up my savings for the wedding suit? The repair was immediately done by a small local garage, to be collected a few days later. The poor little kitten, in the meantime, was not of the luckiest for, during the first night, sleeping in Mrs. A's outside lavatory, it managed to immerse its lower half in the icy water and had to be revived by a quick defrost in Mrs. A's oven: it survived and went on to provide her with the companionship that she was hoping for. It was also treated to the tin of salmon which Margaret had thoughtfully brought along as a special treat for Mrs. A, since tins of salmon were not easy to come by in those days of food rationing: this callous lack of gratitude illustrates fairly graphically why that lady was not one of our favourite people! The Liverpool experience with our three-wheeler led to that car being sold again a few weeks later, at a price which was almost exactly what we had paid for it a year earlier. It was replaced by the Hillman Minx to which I referred above which, in spite of its 20 years of service, was still a very comfortable and sturdy vehicle, having just had a thorough overhaul by Malcolm, a fellow lodger at Mrs. Czyrko's, in preparation for selling the car to us.

CHAPTER
THIRTEEN

Wedding and Honeymoon

The Hillman was a wedding present to ourselves and was very soon to take us up to Scotland on our honeymoon: it, too, led us into some memorable adventures over the next three years. The wedding itself, however, was well prepared and a very special day for us both. All of Margaret's close family from Cleethorpes and Boston was there and, on my side, Mrs. Austin made the journey from Liverpool the day before and stayed with me at Darley's Hotel, where we would be for the reception, as did Michael Abrams, who had agreed to be my best man and did the job extremely well. Mrs. A's sisters, Edith and Nell from the Isle of Man, were already at nearby Lincoln, staying with a family friend who drove them over for the day. Had we wished to include Philip Austin in the guest list, we would have come up against an insuperable obstacle, for he was already incarcerated in Wakefield Prison, having been convicted of paedophilia. The three ladies made up the full complement of my "family" but, since I had long ago appropriated Margaret's family for my own, I certainly had no feeling of being isolated or neglected.

The service was conducted by Herbert Lindley, minister at Beaconthorpe Methodist Church, long a favourite with Margaret and well-known to us both, since he had baptised me when I was enthusiastic about becoming a member of the church and had also been kind enough to invite us for a meal at his home. This forthright northerner with a strong Yorkshire accent knew us well too and his familiarity shone through the wedding service, making it very special. I have mentioned Abie, our best man; Margaret's friend Win and sister Mavis were the chief bridesmaids, as well as Lynne, Stan's young daughter, while nephew Raymond completed the team as pageboy; even the taxi driver who drove us to and from Mill Road Methodist was a friend, Len Burton. A quick look at the wedding photographs, especially those just before the ceremony began, conveys the festive and happy atmosphere of the event, which the photographer captured so well. It was while we were standing grouped on the steps of the church that Margaret overheard one of the bystanders whispering loudly to her neighbour that, "her mother ought to be ashamed of herself, letting a little girl like that get married!" And it is quite true that then, at 23, just as now at 79, it was/is difficult to believe her true age. She looked radiant, and no wonder, given the five years of waiting, planning and sewing her wedding dress and going-away wardrobe.

Darley's Hotel, where the reception had been arranged by Margaret's parents was, in those days (it has gone rather down-at-heel in later years), quite an attractive location and the meal that was served, a standard English salad, was very acceptable. Abie had very thoughtfully brought along a bottle of Veuve Cliquot, which he opened for the select few of us who gathered in the hotel bedroom he and I had shared the night before and which was our changing room before we headed off in our different directions. Aunt Ruby from Boston had also put in some thought, so that, when we went out to the parked cars, our Hillman was covered in good-tempered and helpful suggestions for newly-weds, as well as having the usual crop of tins tied to the rear bumper. Everyone had gathered in the forecourt to wave us off at about 3p.m., the meal and the speeches having been completed in very good time. The remark which I have retained most forcefully from these speeches was made by Margaret's father, not normally renowned for memorable dicta but, on this occasion, very much on the ball: he referred to my recent success in obtaining a first-class degree and added, "I am delighted that I have been able to present you with a first-class wife". Sadly, he was not allowed to stay around long enough to see how accurate he was, for he died of a sudden heart attack less than three years later.

It had been a fine, sunny morning as we prepared for the ceremony and arrived at Mill Road, and it stayed bright even as we drove away from Darley's, leaving all the friends and family behind. However, 15 minutes later, as we were driving along the Laceby Road to leave Grimsby behind, down came the most virulent cloudburst, such that, within minutes, the road was covered in deep pools of water because the drains were totally unable to cope. It was then that I discovered for the first, but certainly not for the last time, that car engines in those more primitive days, when there was little protection under the bonnet for the spark plugs, were very vulnerable to the spray which is thrown up when the car drives through any depth of water. What is more, the 1932 type of windscreen wiper was equally unable to deal with the water rained down in those conditions. Just as suddenly, the sun came back, dried off the spark plugs and we were able to set off once more, heading towards York, where the first two nights of our honeymoon were spent at the appropriately named Chase Hotel. Although the evening was gloomy and wet, we had a stroll around the neighbouring racecourse and then made our way down to the hotel restaurant. We really felt that we had arrived when we were brought melon and ginger for a starter, followed by Maryland chicken, which sounded much grander then than it would strike us nowadays. A visit to Mother Shipton's cave in Knaresborough, followed by a walk round the streets of old York was how we spent the Sunday, before setting off on the trail to Edinburgh the next morning.

The journey north was full of memories for Margaret, as we drove through Wide Open and Pity Me in the Newcastle area near where she had spent her happy teenage years in County Durham. My own inexperience and lack of knowledge of the terrain, however, became increasingly obvious as we climbed up the mountainous road which I had selected for its direct line approach to Edinburgh, ignoring the much safer coast road which looked both longer and more winding on the map. Thus it was that our journey came to an abrupt halt as we turned a sharp left-hand bend with an inverse camber on the road and with a considerable drop on the far side, a drop from which we were fortunately saved by a stretched wire, over which the right mudguard of the Hillman got itself entwined. We sat there stunned for a moment, realising the good fortune which had prevented us from sliding over the edge, for the camber of the road had sent us skidding over to the wrong side and into the path of any oncoming vehicle that there might have been: as luck would have it, the road had remained empty of traffic! In fact, the whole countryside looked as though it was totally empty. As we sat there, wondering what should be done next, and then had a walk round the car to examine the seriousness of our situation, out of the blue, there appeared a man who can only be described as an instinctive officer, who immediately took charge of the situation. Having commanded Margaret to sit tight in the car and keep out of the way, he conjured up one or two foot soldiers out of space and, with a, "Come on, men! Heave!", lifted the car off the wire and sent us gratefully on our way. There was a slight dent in the mudguard, but nothing to cause any great worry.

From then on, the honeymoon went much according to plan, without any further incident of the kind just described, though the daily rain in Scotland did send Margaret off in search of more solid footwear.

Edinburgh, of course, had much to offer then as it does now and we were greatly impressed with our room at the Roxburgh Hotel, huge by present-day standards and quite amazing when, as we rediscovered recently when looking through old photographs and memorabilia, the tariff for a night was a mere eight shillings and six pence for bed and breakfast.

The weather continued gloomy as we drove further north through Glencoe to reach Fort William, where we were due to spend our second week at the Highland Hotel on an all-in basis. We shared a table with two delightful Scottish spinster ladies who guessed that we were on our honeymoon, in spite of our every effort to cover up this secret, and enjoyed looking after us. It was here that we were introduced to the delights of venison with its rich gravy and, on our coach tour to Inverness, to fresh salmon, a much rarer delicacy then compared with its easy availability now that we have farmed salmon in all our supermarkets. No complaints, therefore, about the food that we were served, but the beds were another story: the mattresses and pillows were the main topic of the questions asked of the "Brains Trust" at the question and answer session held at the end of the week, the conclusion being that they were stuffed with heather! No doubt about it, though, we learned a lot about the Highlands and the Lochs during that week and, overall, we were left with many happy memories to take back to Cleethorpes and then to Leicester, when it was time for Margaret to rejoin her school.

CHAPTER
FOURTEEN

Back to the Grind

I have already described in some detail the work that Margaret was expected to do with her "specials" at High Cross School. It must have been depressing for her to go back to that dismal task without even the comfort of knowing that she had to endure only one more term, but it was love and the wish to stay in Leicester with me that kept her going. Not only was she expected to cope with the numbers and the range of ages referred to above, but she had to deal with the full range of subjects, including Religious Education, basic Maths, everything, because the only other teacher in the school willing to have the group was our friend Lorna, who took them on for Singing and Music. Gradually, too, all her breaks and lunch hour were whittled away, as her miserable Head insisted that these girls be supervised all through the day and nobody else on the staff was prepared to step in. Looking back at it now, from the point of view of an experienced Head of many years, dealing with children of all abilities and all types, I just find myself incredulous at what she was asked to live through with those girls. It is hardly surprising, then, that, by October in the 4th term, she was at the end of her tether and sufficiently visibly so that, when she bumped into the Primary Schools Adviser in the street (she knew Margaret because of a night-school class of Nursery Nurses, whom Margaret was teaching English in order to keep her sanity!), this lady advised her to put in her notice and promised her a job with a reception class at Harrison Road Primary. What a relief and what a change in her life, since she absolutely adored that group of children and found them and the work to be a pure delight. After High Cross School and its misery, as I said earlier, nothing would ever again trouble her, because nothing in her professional life would ever again be as bad! There was one other good result which emerged from those first four terms — our friendship with Lorna and Eric Waller, which lasted until their sad and premature deaths.

All of the above took place as a consequence of our returning to Leicester as a married couple to the same house where Margaret and Win had shared the ground floor flat, whereas we now moved to the top floor, where we had a living room and a bedroom under the eaves, with a washing-up bowl on the landing for our dishes, but the kitchen was two floors down and the bathroom was on the floor below. Sadly, Mrs. Gisborne, who had been such a help to Margaret with her sewing was, by that time, in hospital with terminal cancer. However, we were happily installed and free to bring our own, novel decorating ideas into action: my first attempt at wallpaper hanging took the roll up the wall, across the sloping and flat parts of the ceiling and, non-stop, down the other side. I was fortunate to have help from John Rutt (a College friend in the Science Faculty) with the paper hanging, since going over ceilings is always a problem — a sad memory since John died so tragically a couple of years afterwards, when he was struck on the temple by a cricket ball. Very early on, we threw our first party, inviting friends from the two year groups that I had been involved with, as well as any who had been missed out from our wedding celebrations. The numbers we crowded into that space were such that it was very difficult to move and difficult also to find one's mouth with the good things that Margaret had prepared: as a result, the room looked like a pigsty after the gathering and the cleaning-up operation was tedious, but a good time was had by all.

My own experience of cookery was pretty limited at that time, even with ready-made products in tins. On one famous occasion, I left a tin of steak and kidney pudding warming on Mrs. Gisborne's stove in a pan of boiling water, not realising that these things are better pierced. Fortunately, neither of us was in the kitchen when the pan boiled dry and the tin exploded; Mrs. G, of course, was in hospital. The kitchen, as you can imagine, was thoroughly bespattered and needed to be cleaned from floor to ceiling.

With all its inconveniences, that top-floor flat provided us with a good home for two terms and even had its own parking space on the paved area just round the corner on Queen's Road. Here "Niv", as we called our car because of its NV registration, stood happily, waiting for me to crank it up in the mornings. Up would go the driver's side of the bonnet so that I could reach the choke control on the carburettor and then I would give the crank handle a hefty turn, trying, not always successfully, to keep my tie out of the fan belt, and off it would go, the engine usually being fairly compliant. Like most drivers of such cars, I did learn a fair amount about internal combustion engines, which served very little purpose once we progressed to the more modern and sophisticated engines in the later 50s.

The winter of 52/3 was quite severe, especially in the New Year, when I was travelling daily to Market Harborough for my teaching practice. Having my own means of transport to get me there was, of course, very convenient, but the early morning starting up of my engine, followed by the freezing up of the windscreen as I drove through the Leicestershire countryside, could be quite harrowing. The time factor was made more important by the fact that I was giving a lift to two or three other students doing their practice at the same school or the nearby Secondary Modern, each of whom was making a contribution to the petrol. Only someone familiar with pre-war cars can possibly understand the demands of not just turning a key or a switch to start the car, of having no car heater in the depth of winter to keep the windscreen from steaming or freezing up and of relying on a little electric motor to work the wipers which, if the motor is being temperamental, have to be operated by hand while, at the same time, keeping the car safely on the road. Having read about these difficulties, the modern reader would be tempted to ask why we had to put up with such an old vehicle? The answer lies in the knowledge of the times: banks then did not offer borrowing facilities to the working man or the student, quite apart from which Margaret's upbringing, highly charged with her mother's fear of debt and borrowing, other than for a house mortgage, would not have allowed her even to think about it. And a very healthy attitude I recognise that to have been, knowing the sort of situation that a happy-go-lucky young man like me might have been manoeuvred into.

In school, at Market Harborough Grammar School, I immediately fell into a groove. The pupils accepted me quite happily and worked hard for me; the recommended techniques seemed to fall into place and I enjoyed myself in the classroom. The French teacher whose classes I was mainly taking over was happy to retire into the background and left me to get on with things, even with his examination classes. My tutors came and went and seemed to think that all was well and discipline was no problem with these pleasant, rural children. Even Professor Tibble came and sat in happily on one or two of my classes. All in all, Market Harborough was a pleasure and fully confirmed me in thinking that teaching was going to be a good career for a confident and ambitious young man.

The whole year was carefree also, in the sense that we knew where we were planning to go once it was completed: we had agreed that the Certificat de Licence which I had passed at Rennes should be added to and the Licence finished off by returning to France for a second year as "assistant". This time, we hoped, I would be allocated a school in a University town, enabling me to avoid the travelling that I had been forced to undertake between St. Brieuc and Rennes. Toulouse, therefore, was an ideal placing for me, but we were not to know that my gain would turn out to be Margaret's loss for, when she was eventually allocated a school, it was in Auch, at a distance of 80 kilometres away.

Well before our departure to France, however, Mrs. Gisborne's long drawn-out illness finally led to her death in the spring of 1953, followed by the clearing of her house ready for sale. We soon found another convenient flat with a delightful spinster lady, just round the corner from the Queen's Road shops that we were thoroughly familiar with and, although the kitchen corner of the living area was only orange boxes behind a curtain, the two rooms that we had were light and spacious and we were happy there.

Teaching in a primary school had eased Margaret's life considerably for, although she was always very thorough in her preparation, it was as nothing compared with that class of 28 all-age "specials". For my part, the last month or two of the education year, once the various pieces of written work had been disposed of, were scarcely hectic. Very soon, therefore, while Margaret's school year went on until the second half of July, I was able to launch into a paid holiday job to start earning towards our travelling expenses on our way down to Toulouse. Already, during that summer term, I remember dealing with Margaret's complaint, repeated again and again in later life, that I was neglecting my wife by allowing long periods of silence when I was reading or otherwise occupied, by taking up stitching rugs which, in a year or two, would be stretched in front of our hearth in Castle Bromwich. I am still far from sure that this peaceful activity led to any greater contribution from me to the evening's conversation but, over the years, it led me into a hobby which produced some interesting pieces of handicraft, progressing from those rugs, through embroidery and Hardanger work, to the tapestries which are now decorating the living-room wall.

Because we were young and carefree, we had, as far as I can recall, no misgivings about where the next year in France was going to lead us. There was no long-term strategy and we had no particular preference for where to settle on our return: had we been told that our home was going to be in Birmingham, I doubt whether we would have been easily convinced, for neither of us had spent any time there and the picture in our minds would, no doubt, have been of an industrial and grimy city. Before that, however, we had August and September in Cleethorpes, as always, earning as much as we could to give us a springboard, but with a fortnight of real holiday, shared with Mavis and her husband Steve, in our adventurous car, which was soon to take us across the Channel to Toulouse. Mavis and Steve had married in the April before our wedding and, as was so often the case in those days, were living with Steve's parents until they had enough for a deposit to put on a little bungalow. Steve was a fully qualified bricklayer and, although I am sure that he was earning good money, had no car at that stage, with the result that they were quite eager to take advantage of the offer to share a camping tour with us.

CHAPTER
FIFTEEN

A Camping Holiday
for Four

It was before the days of roof racks and our dear old
Hillman offered only the fold-down rack on its tail,
with our large, green cabin trunk strapped on for
everything we might wish to take though, of course, the
couple sitting in the back would not escape having to
put up with some paraphernalia. Quite apart from all
our clothing for the holiday, we had to find space for
two small two-man tents, two safari beds which offered
approximately 2ft 6inches of sleeping space for each
couple inside the tents, a little petrol stove for heating
the kettle and pan, sufficient food to feed ourselves at
breakfast time and, of course, bedding for the nights
which could be chilly. If all of the above arrangements
make it sound terribly crowded and rather sparse, that
is precisely how it was and, since it was intended all to
be on a shoestring budget, our tour of the Midlands
and the South West was, nevertheless, quite surprisingly
enjoyable for all concerned. Not only did we see what
was quite new to us in Stratford, Leamington and
Gloucester, the Forest of Dean, along the Somerset

coast down to Torquay and Lyme Regis, before turning north again to Salisbury and Oxford, but we managed to find cheap cafes and eating places, all of which offered us roast beef and Yorkshire pudding!

Our camping places were often unusual, providing little in the way of facilities, but sometimes memorable for the character of their owner, as in the case of the midwife, Mrs. Rice, in whose garden we set up our tents under her watchful eye. She was most intrigued with the bacon that we were frying on our little petrol stove and not satisfied until she had forced us into confessing that we had more bacon than our normal rations would allow, because it came from Mum, who had Pop's extra ration for being a diabetic! The same lady was most anxious to take down our car registration number and promised to keep her ears open to catch any radio emergency messages that might follow on our being involved in an accident! Later in the holiday, when we were camping in a field belonging to the village pub, the girls eventually plucked up the courage to go with us and order a "gin and orange" — "I won't tell Mum if you don't!" — the courage being necessary to overcome the fear of what Mum might think and say, rather than the actual going into the pub.

The last night of the holiday, perhaps because the money in the kitty was getting rather low, was spent on a racecourse in Oxfordshire where there were no facilities, but it was free. It was then that my resourceful wife produced the £5 note she had secreted from all our eyes and said we should treat ourselves to a farewell

110

dinner at the nearby "posh" hotel at Weston-on-the-Green. However, before we dared enter the dining room, Steve and I felt that we had to clean ourselves up and make ourselves presentable by having a shave in the cloakroom. That was easier said than done, since electric shaver points were then much rarer than they are now. There was nothing else for it but for me to climb onto Steve's shoulders to reach the electric light socket and, of course, it was just at that moment that the door opened to admit a shocked guest! I mumbled something like, "It's terribly difficult to get a shave around here!" and then we carried on. The meal in the restaurant was as good as it promised, but poor Steve, who, having little experience of eating out, was rather overawed by the occasion, with the result that, when the waiter was serving the garden peas to accompany the gammon, stayed silent while the plate was piled higher and higher until the serving dish was completely empty, not realising that it was up to him to say "thank you" when he had had enough. "He needn't think that I'm eating all these peas!", he then said, while the rest of us collapsed into fits of laughter: a fitting end to a memorable holiday, in which there had been just one unfortunate incident.

On the beach in Torquay Mavis, always a keen swimmer, was dying to get in the water and had been helped in her disrobing by Margaret, who held a large towel around her while she changed. Poor Steve, who was rather narrow-minded in outlook, thought this procedure was dreadful and refused to speak to Mavis for the rest of that day and the next, which did rather create an atmosphere that could be cut with a knife. The night in Lyme Regis was also rather special, for we arrived at the campsite in pouring rain, which did not let up all evening and most of the night. None of us was courageous enough to try and put up the tents in this rain, so we slept, or rather tried to sleep, in our seats in the car, which steamed up and smelled extremely stale by the morning. We drove off without making any attempt to pay the campsite fee for the night, so that helped!

CHAPTER
SIXTEEN

An Eventful Year
in Toulouse

Not long after this excursion and whatever holiday job I had managed to sort out in Cleethorpes — as a lemonade salesman, driving my lorry to all the seaside eateries along the Promenade — it was time to set off for France in our faithful Hillman Minx which, when all was done, looked as though we really had packed everything including the kitchen sink. There being no motorways, the journey down to Folkestone and then on the French roads was much more laborious than it is now. With a maximum speed of around 45/50 mph, there had to be a careful plan, with a hotel booked at the end of every day's journey. Crossing the Channel with a car was also very different from the roll-on roll-off ferries that we are now accustomed to. Seeing your car being hoisted 30 metres into the air and then lowered onto the deck of the ferry, with the reverse taking place at the end of the journey onto the quayside at Boulogne, is a picture which stays firmly printed on your memory. I can well remember the thoughts that ran through my mind, as to what would be the result if the crane should happen to drop its precious load. There were also lengthy documents to be filled in for the English and then the French authorities. Soon, though, we were on the dockside at Boulogne, explaining to the douaniers why we were travelling with a Singer sewing machine in our rear compartment. They were so convinced that we had brought it specifically to sell at a great profit to some unsuspecting French housewife that I had to sign a document, promising that we would still have the machine for re-export when we came to leave the country the following July. There were other items, too, in our car and in the trunk that was always strapped onto our rack which intrigued the French Customs, who were quite unused to people coming to spend long periods in their country. Eventually though, we managed to satisfy their curiosity and were able to set off.

After a night in Pontoise, followed by one in Chateauroux, we came to Bergerac, where poor Margaret had an adventure outside our hotel bedroom. She spotted a little mouse fluttering about, with the result that, when I came up to collect our overnight suitcase, I found her standing on a table, skirt pulled tightly round her legs, making sure that, if the mouse had followed her in, it certainly would not have been able to reach her.

Once I had been informed that Toulouse was going to be my posting for the year 1953/4, Adrien Favre, who had so conveniently had his brother's family at Rennes when I was in St. Brieuc, once again came to our assistance by having a good contact in Toulouse,

114

who ran a Commercial College in the town. M. Billieres, his friend, offered us his rural retreat in the village of Lardenne, on the outskirts of Toulouse, in return for a one-hour evening class in English, which Margaret was to teach to an unknown group of adults one evening per week. This seemed a very manageable arrangement to us, since it would provide us with a more or less cost-free home for our time in Toulouse. Unfortunately, the house did not become available until November 1st, meaning that we had to find a month's accommodation for October. My own efforts through the University student bureau came up trumps with a small flat which would tide us over and it was there that we arrived, ready for me to start at the College with my classes of boys. Soon also, I was able to sort out my courses at the University, so as to attain the principal objective of our coming back to France: the completion of my French qualification, the Licence-ès-lettres. Fortunately, our expectation for the flat was not high, for it consisted of a bare-board bedsit, with two or three chairs and a table as well as the bed and a small kitchen, where the sink provided our only rudimentary washing and "bathing" facility. The lavatory, as so often in France, was outside on the landing and was shared with the other flats on that floor. Although the bed was the only piece of furniture in the room which allowed for any relaxation, our youth and lack of expectation of any luxuries allowed us to take all of this in our stride.

We used our leisure time to familiarise ourselves with the city: its famous pinkish buildings and fountains, the theatre and library and, above all the central market

115

and shops. There was a large Monoprix, which tended to offer most products, including food, at the sort of prices that we could afford. Knowing that we would have to fend for ourselves for the first month, until such time as my first month's salary became available, we had saved hard to cover the expense, not only of the hotels and fuel for the journey from the Channel, but also for our immediate needs during the month of October: these included cheap pots and pans, together with food, selected from the cheapest sources.

Disaster struck three weeks or so into the year, while we were still at this student flat when, very suddenly, on one of my school days, as we were eating something with sprouts on the plate, Margaret had a violent stomach upset. In my usual over-confident manner, I diagnosed her problem as a combination of home sickness, from which she was certainly suffering because she was not sufficiently occupied, and indigestion, for which I prescribed a dose of bicarbonate of soda, which succeeded in making her feel very much worse! As a result of this treatment, by the time I returned after my afternoon classes, she was feeling dreadful and rolling on the bed in terrible agony which could not be ignored. A consultation with the concierge, whom we had found on previous occasions to be both sympathetic and helpful, put me in touch with local doctors, the first two of whom blankly refused to come and see someone who was as transient as we were. The third, a Polish gentleman, came directly and ordered me to transport my wife to a Clinique, judging the local hospital to be too risky for a damsel in severe distress. I am quite certain that he was right about the hospital, but the Clinique was first-rate and, shortly after our evening arrival, and an immediate examination by the doctor on duty, I saw my Margaret being wheeled away to the operating theatre, where the surgeon in charge, called away from his evening at home, was waiting to deal with her problem. It was peritonitis and, thanks to me and my bicarbonate of soda, there was little time to spare!

I can't recall how many hours exactly she was in the theatre, but it was a nail-biting time during which I could only think with a high degree of trepidation of how I was going to explain to her mother that I had failed in my duty of caring for her daughter. Imagine my relief when she was wheeled back in and the operation was pronounced a success by the surgeon, proudly bearing her inflamed appendix in a glass jar which he offered to us to be kept as an heirloom. What followed was, "Nothing to eat or drink for three days", not even teeth to be cleaned, in case any water filtered through! Although she enjoyed the luxury of a private room with nurses occasionally putting their head round the door, by the time the three days had gone by, Margaret was more than ready, not only for something to drink but, even more urgently, for an opportunity to get washed. Visiting, on the other hand, was no problem and I could spend all my free time with her, eventually also enjoying any surplus food which might be brought in by the nurse or, for that matter, what was left on the plate and could not be managed by the patient. Difficult though it may be to believe, the first solid food that was brought in was a steak, grilled in the way that any good Frenchman would like it so that, when Margaret cut into it and the blood ran out, there was no question about whose mouth it would end in — mine, of course! There was one other puzzle when Margaret came out of the theatre: her stitches, because operations were not "keyhole" in those days, extended well below her midriff and then were rounded off by a large safety pin, or even a blanket pin, with a little tube protruding underneath. Being total novices when it came to operations, we neither of us could believe that this was an intentional part of a surgical intervention, but the nurse soon informed us, with a very Toulouse accent, that it was a "drain" to allow any fluid from the affected area to escape. The surgeon, when he spoke to me about his findings when Margaret was opened up, had been most impressed by Margaret's pelvic muscles and, being a great rugby enthusiast, said it was little wonder that the English team had convincingly outplayed the French in a recent match, when their womenfolk had such impressive muscles! Though the total recovery took rather longer, I was allowed to remove the patient after a few days, by which time the villa in Lardenne was available to us and Margaret was not obliged to return to our temporary flat, where she would have found the stairs a trial.

There was a longer-lasting legacy from the peritonitis: the adhesions which doctors later found in Margaret's pelvic area and which occasionally reminded her of their presence. More immediately, however, there arose the question of payment for the doctor and the clinic. We are so spoiled in this country by having the NHS to fall back on that it comes as quite a shock when payment is demanded, even though the French system does provide for 70-80% of the costs to be recovered from the Securite Sociale after payment has been made. Here, I must ask you to bear in mind that we had been in France just a month and had been living, up to that point, on the francs that we were able to muster from our holiday earnings, as we waited eagerly for the end of the month to collect my first salary. When it came to the last day and there was still no sign of a cheque either in the post or at school, we literally did not have the proverbial "sou", the larder was empty except for a potato and the petrol gauge in the car was registering zero.

We were out in Lardenne, six miles from the centre of town, knowing nobody and Margaret was laid up with no alternative but to rest. The last day had happened to fall on a Saturday and we were facing a weekend of starvation, so there was nothing for it but to walk into Toulouse, go to my school and see what could be done about my pay. Nothing in my pigeon-hole, nobody in the Econome's office, the building was empty, since it was now after 12 noon. I was just about to walk disconsolately away, with that dreadful feeling that men must have when they are coming home knowing that they have nothing with which to feed their family, when I heard footsteps on the stone floor of the corridor. My luck had changed: it was M. le Directeur, who could see from my face that I was not my usual happy self. When I explained my sorry situation, he

119

dipped into his wallet, took out 2000 francs (the equivalent of £2 at that time, but "manna from heaven!") and sent me off to buy what I needed for the weekend. £2 may not sound much, but it allowed me to buy a small piece of pork, some vegetables and a tin of fruit and I even had sufficient left to allow myself the luxury of going back to Lardenne on the bus instead of walking.

The next question, then, was how to pay the medical expenses. Current income was certainly not likely to exceed current expenditure by much, so I turned once again to the helpful Student Comite d'Accueil, who came to our rescue by lending me the money. Armed with all the receipts, a day or two later, I went to the Social Security to ask for whatever was coming as a refund. We should, of course, have realised that nothing was likely to be straightforward and that minor French officialdom was there principally to make life difficult. "Sorry, it is laid down in the regulations that you cannot make a claim until you have been working for a full month!" No amount of pleading, explaining our situation or arguing that it would all have been free on the NHS, with health care in France being, supposedly, reciprocal, brought us any closer to sorting the matter out.

Over the whole of October and November the same rigmarole took place every week when we went in to argue: to no avail. Naturally, Margaret was not slow to complain to her mother in her letters about what was going on and it was Mum who took the initiative, went to see the local MP, Cyril Osborne (all hail to his memory!), who knew something about the reciprocity which, nominally, had been negotiated between the English and the French systems and followed it up. One fine day in December, therefore, when we went in to have our regular session of argument with the officials, we were suddenly shocked by the complete collapse of opposition: "Hold on! We are going to pay you", she said, as we nearly fainted with the shock and, money in hand, rushed out of the office before anyone could have a change of heart.

With that, the debt could be paid off, but we were still far from well off, living, as we were, on one not-very-generous salary. It was then that we had a real stroke of luck. One of the very good things about Toulouse was the American Library, to which we returned every few days, because it kept both of us supplied with good reading, whereas we had found the British Council library to be rather bare and unimaginative in its stock. The American Library also arranged regular talks by academics who came and expounded on appropriate literary topics. The November talk, which we were happy to go along and hear, was given by a very kind Professor of English who, after his lecture on *Romeo and Juliet*, stayed on to meet the "assistants" and to hear how they found things after two months in France. Margaret and I took the opportunity to pour out our woes to him — this was before the Social Security had had their change of heart — and told him about the Ministry of Education's apparent difficulty in finding a place for Margaret in any of the local schools. I think that he felt distinctly sorry for us, especially when he heard about Margaret's recent operation and he said: "I think that my country has treated you very shabbily. I shall have a word with M. Renard, the Minister, about it and we shall see what he can do". That was our first experience of what the French call "piston", where personal influence can be exerted to produce the desired result, proving that who you know is often much more effective than what you know. He must have kept his word and swiftly for, almost by the end of the week, we had a letter from the Ministry offering Margaret the post of "assistante" at the College de Jeunes Filles at Auch, a market town about 50 miles NW of Toulouse, whereas our previous repeated requests had been met only with Gerardmer, a lovely place, but hundreds of miles away in the Vosges. Better still, the railway line up to Auch passed directly through our village station of Lardenne, which meant that she could catch the train without going in to the centre of Toulouse. Of course, she was delighted to accept, even though it meant an hour and a half's journey on a slow train, leaving the village at 6a.m. and getting back late in the afternoon: we felt as though things had begun to go right for us at long last.

Toulouse at Christmas was not the merriest of places, for we had not made too many friends during that troubled period and we spent much of our time in the house, reading and, in my case, studying for the two Certificates I would be taking at the end of the year. Nevertheless, there were contacts with other "assistants", some being there, like us, for the year only, others, like M. Baro, the Spanish assistant at my school,

122

permanently settled — being a refugee from the time of the Spanish Civil War in the 30s. We also met other expatriates at the American Library and it was one of these, an English lady married to a Frenchman, who invited us to her house for a "proper" Christmas dinner, which we looked forward to. When we arrived at her house, we were invited into the living room which was freezing cold but, for our benefit, she brought in a small, ancient-looking one-bar electric fire, which she placed in the middle of the room and which had absolutely no effect on the overall temperature. Because she was working in the kitchen, we were left very much to our own devices, since her husband failed to put in an appearance. She then came back briefly to remove the fire which was needed, we were told, to take the chill off the dining room, to which we were to be invited shortly. When, eventually, we transferred, the husband appeared, sensibly wearing a beret to keep his head warm, and offered us a welcome which was, in every respect, as chilly as the house. The Boxing Day dinner I cannot remember.

Our own house at Lardenne was not much warmer, but could be heated in one of two ways, the principal being the metal horse-type stove in the kitchen, in which we burned "boules" of compressed coal dust. This had the advantage of throwing out heat into the relatively cosy, but comfortless kitchen and, at the same time, heating a kettle or a pan on its "seat". Upstairs, in our improvised living area, where two wicker chairs provided the height of comfort, there was a large open fireplace in the corner, where we tried the occasional wood fire, only to discover that, as the chimney rose vertically to the roof, the slightest puff of wind would blow the smoke straight back down the chimney and into our faces: thus, we were not too keen on open fires.

Apart from the lack of comfort and the paucity of furniture in the house, the most striking feature in my memory is the wallpaper in the two upstairs rooms. It was geometrical in the extreme, of a type which, to my knowledge, was totally unknown in England and which, to say the least, was eye dazzling and not easy to live with. What is more, the French way of papering — we have seen the same approach both at Daniel and Yolande's and in properties belonging to friends in Rotary at Brest — is to cover doors and cupboards without any break or differentiation, so that they become indistinguishable from the wall itself. The result is a constant puzzle for the untrained eye, which finds it extremely difficult to see the doors when they are closed. This was especially so in our living room where, in addition to the normal door onto the landing, there was also the attached washing area — not a bathroom, I hasten to say, but a simple washstand, to which water had to be brought in a tall enamel jug from the only source of running water in the house: the kitchen tap. And, of course, there had to be a bucket for the waste water to be emptied away. When that door was closed, it became part of the wall, especially as its handle was a small semi-circular ring, set into the door itself, with the entire wall being a blue, gold and white criss-cross of shapes, while the bedroom had different shapes, with red and cream as the dominant colours.

Life was not easy in Lardenne, but we didn't expect it to be. The huge advantage of the house was that we were independent and it was totally affordable since, as has been said before, the rent was paid by Margaret giving her weekly lesson at Billieres' establishment in Toulouse. We fully expected to make do with whatever we were given and, if that meant cooking on a two-ring stove for a year, then so be it. Eat we did and, usually, we managed a weekend joint. The limitations also led Margaret into tasty improvisations like the apple turnovers cooked in the chip pan with boiling fat. Had it not been for our car, life would have been much more complicated, as we discovered when some kind person walking down our lane decided to remove the petrol cap, leaving the semi-vertical petrol filler pipe open to the elements and the petrol, inevitably, becoming unusable after a night of rain. Fortunately, I was able to borrow a bicycle from a colleague at school, until such time as the car became mobile once more by having the tank drained and refilled. It was, of course, at the very worst of the weather that all of this took place, for that winter was as severe as the people of Toulouse had ever known: not only did domestic water pipes freeze, but the fountains for which the city is rightly famous froze solid and I have never seen icicles so long and so thick! In spite of deep snow, Margaret continued her commuting to Auch, even though she had to be transported to the station on the crossbar of my borrowed bicycle: hazardous at the best of times, but leading to great discomfort when the bicycle slid away from under me at the turning for the station at

Lardenne. A snow bath at 6 in the morning is not our idea of beginning the day well, even less is it likely to lead to a comfortable ride on the train for the next hour and a half!

The coming of spring and early summer eased those particular problems considerably. We could stop worrying about heating and the washing that Margaret did in a zinc bath on a gas ring could be hung outside instead of being draped across the kitchen. At long last also, we were able to derive some benefit and pleasure from the garden, even though it had to be neglected for want of implements. The wall at the far end of the garden separated us from the neighbouring family of a mother and two sons, whose land was a little personal vineyard and who lived in the still quite primitive conditions associated with rural areas in the France of those days. A glance through the open door of their kitchen was a revelation of how French peasants lived — in fact, 40 years later, when we were searching for a property in Brittany, we still came across pretty similar households. Our first contact with that family was when one of the young men came to ask for our permission to collect snails from our wall after some heavy rain: it was quite easy to say "yes". It was they also who said that we must not think about a Monoprix chicken for our Christmas dinner — far better to have a farm bird that they would find for us. It turned out to be a scrawny, yellowish thing that we had to clean out in our urban, inexperienced way, while wondering whether they would have eaten it with all its entrails still inside?

CHAPTER
SEVENTEEN

A Busy French Summer

As summer drew nearer, I had, of course, to think about a job for the following year, something which, if my memory serves me at all well, we had given no serious thought to before going to France. The first thing was to arrange for the *Times Educational Supplement* to be sent over and then, having skimmed through all the vacancies quickly, to make certain that any applications I sent would reach their destination before the closing date. That, in itself, was quite demanding and had to be followed by a rapid decision as to which interviews I could afford to attend, in view of the inevitable restriction that travel expenses would only be refunded from the English Channel port. The outcome was that I selected two consecutive days when I could attend first the Tiffin Boys' School in Kingston-on-Thames, a very reputable Independent Grammar School, always placed very high in the results table, with the back-up of two further interviews in Birmingham on the following day, just in case I did not get the job in Kingston. The two in Birmingham were at Bordesley Green and Handsworth Technical Schools, intermediate schools with a 13+ entry, for boys who were being given a second chance, having failed the 11+.

The afternoon at Kingston started at 2p.m. in the traditional manner, with a long chat first with the Head, followed by a long tête-à-tête with his No. 2, who then passed me over to the Head of Modern Languages, all very friendly and pursuing various lines of enquiry, ranging from my family history to my ideas on the teaching of French at this level. There was no one else being interviewed that afternoon, so it was proceeding in a leisurely manner and, at 4.30, was still not concluded. Eventually, I was passed back to the Head, who was an ex-Brigadier, with a fairly military manner to go with it and who returned to the subject of my foreign extraction and background. All in all, he was saying, because my mother and sisters died at the hands of the Germans and because of my being orphaned, I must, therefore, hate the Germans and could not teach French and German without being affected by that hatred! The outcome was that he could not possibly appoint me and my reply to him was that, after hearing what he had to say, I should have been most reluctant to accept the post.

So, off I went to Birmingham, quite determined not to return to Toulouse without a job. I managed to have a quick look at both schools in the morning and, having had rather longer with Bertie Brown at Bordesley, who wanted French to be started from scratch, with new textbooks to be chosen, and who was prepared to offer all sorts of inducements in order to capture a man with a 1st Class Honours degree, I accepted Bordesley Green in the afternoon: quite apart from anything else, the buildings at Handsworth were ancient and dilapidated and the school had no playing fields, whereas there was a field and a running track at Bordesley. What is more, I had been introduced to one of the staff who had, on frequent occasions, been prepared to let half his house to young couples like us, so that we were spared the nuisance of flat hunting for September: we were booked in at the 3Ds', Don, Doris and Doreen, their 10-year old daughter, with only Margaret's teaching post to sort out before we started.

With the academic year drawing to a close, it was, of course, time for those University examinations which had been the main incentive for us to spend the extra year in France. I absolutely had to pass the two further Certificats de Licence which, when added to the Philology I had passed in Rennes, would entitle me to the Licence. This additional qualification would distinguish me from the many other candidates with good degrees with whom I would be competing for promotion. Naturally, therefore, on our arrival in Toulouse, I had immediately enrolled at the University for a course I found attractive and which was suitable for the degree combination: Meridional Language and Literature, in other words the early French of the South, which later disappeared when the North became dominant. For the other course, I was given a free choice and I selected American Literature and Civilisation, thinking that here was an opportunity for me to have a fairly easy passage because of my language advantage. So confident was I of being able to deal easily with the American course that I decided to take full advantage of the French University set-up, which allows you to present yourself for the end-of-year exams without necessarily having attended any of the lectures. Thus, I concentrated assiduously on the course in Meridional Studies, following the lectures and presenting all the course work, just as I had done in Rennes, whereas I just did the necessary set reading for the American course, expecting it to be a walkover when it actually came to the exam. Looking back on it now, it was really quite predictable that pride came before what was very nearly a disastrous fall since, had I not obtained both Certificats, there would have been no Licence and the year would, in that respect, have been wasted. As I explained earlier, the French system gives one no choice in the questions set for an exam at this level: there is a narrow slip of paper with one question and four hours in which to show the examiner what you know. Imagine my dismay when I read the slip for American Literature and found myself faced with a question on Walt Whitman's *Leaves of Grass*, a book of poetry which did not appear on my list of texts to be studied. I had, perfectly properly, followed the printed syllabus published at the beginning of the academic year and had my ideas about Hemingway, Dos Passos and Thoreau's *Walden or Life in the Woods*, but I had never read one word of Walt Whitman. How I did it, I do not know, but I wrote for over three hours about those poems that I had never read and then came out of the exam hall feeling as though my world had collapsed around me. I can't remember exactly what Margaret said to me when I described my morning, but she was not pleased and who can blame her? She had spent the year, as I had, working for a pittance instead of a proper teacher's salary, with very little comfort and some unhappiness and now it looked as though there would be nothing to show for all that.

With my tail between my legs, I scampered back to the University that afternoon, bearing with me the booklet with the list of set books that they had issued at the beginning of the year. There was not much that could be done at the Registry, but they gave me the address of the lecturer in charge of the course and suggested that I went to see him, which I did. He came to the door, he listened to my tale of woe and, being his own master, he decided that I was not without some justification and, if I came back three days later, he would set me a question on the syllabus that I had studied. That, in itself, was a relief, but greater relief followed when the set question turned out to be on Thoreau, whom I did know thoroughly and was able to write about with great competence. The outcome of all this living on a knife-edge? I was awarded good passes in both papers and my Licence-és-lettres was there for me to take back to England and add to my English qualifications. Did it make any difference to the way that I was regarded by future potential employers? Who knows? But I would not have enjoyed being in my shoes and having to face up to my wife had the result been different!

With the academic year now over, we prepared for our journey home, which was planned to take us east through Carcassonne, with its memorable, ancient city walls, to Aix and Avignon and up the Rhone valley. My friend from Brittany, Herve, now married to Misette, whom he had met when they were both working in Derby, was now teaching in the French-administered part of West Germany, in the ancient city of Trier or Treves, and had invited us to come and spend a few days with them in the Moselle valley, before continuing our journey home to England. This seemed an excellent idea, for neither Margaret nor I had ever spent any time in the east of France and it would allow us to take full advantage of our car and our well-placed friends. We were much impressed by the beautiful scenery of the Moselle valley and Herve was a delightful host: unfortunately, we did not get on quite so well with Misette, who was always anxious to show that little bit of superiority.

The remainder of the journey took us through Namur and into Brussels, where we planned to stop a day or two. It was in Namur that we famously spent a "dirty" night as an unmarried couple when we overnighted in a little bar/hotel, where the waiter doubled as receptionist. The formalities in the 50s were rather more demanding than now and, when we showed him our passports, the waiter saw Mrs. T. M. Austin on Margaret's, but Alfred Stiller alias Austin on mine, so he insisted in his hotel book that our room was shared by Mrs. Austin with Mr. Stiller — an anecdote we have related many times and which never fails to raise a smile. Our arrival in Brussels the next day was perhaps even more memorable, though it could easily have been serious had my luck not held firm. Our ancient Hillman, now 22 years old, had begun to show signs of "bits dropping off" (as they do, when one reaches a certain age!) in the Rhone valley, when water began to come through the floorboards on the passenger side and the spoked wheels took exception to the cobbled streets of northern France and Belgium, occasionally going PING!, as another spoke broke or departed. We were heading for a cheap hotel by the Gare du Nord in central Brussels and going downhill on a cobbled street behind a single-decker bus when the brake rod snapped — NO BRAKES! Thank goodness we were already going fairly slowly, as we headed for a cross roads controlled by a white-gloved policeman, and the Hillman bumper, proper metal on those models, did not make too much of an impression on the back of the bus, whose driver didn't even get out to have a look. Hastily, I took the next right in order to get off the main road, only to be confronted by another white-gloved policeman, who was gesticulating wildly because it happened to be a one-way street in the wrong direction! I explained that I had no brakes and that we were only going to the hotel round the corner, so he waved us on and sighed loudly, "Ah, ces Anglais!" As luck had it, right next door to our hotel, which we reached without further incident, there was a little garage of the good, old-fashioned, primitive kind where, for a few francs, they were able to weld our brake system together and make us roadworthy again, though I would never have been able to get through an MOT. Having had a good look round the city and after finding such important landmarks as the "Maneken Pis", we set off again towards the coast by way of Ghent, spending our last few cents on a bag of chips from a stall in the beautiful Town Hall Square, before going on to Ostend for the boat.

Once more, we saw the Minx being craned high overhead and swung onto the boat, before we set off on the four-hour crossing to Dover and then on to London, where we stayed the night with Win's family in Southwark — the only flat that I had ever seen with an inside staircase leading up to the extra bedrooms that accommodated Win and her five sisters. London to Grimsby was still quite a distance and the wheels, having lost some of their spokes, could be heard squeakily protesting and still losing the odd spoke, even on good English roads. Our final tribulation was a puncture about 10 miles out of Grimsby, with the wheel having to be changed in the dark. Off came the trunk which always sat on the luggage rack at the back of the car, nestling against the spare wheel, the whole scene being "floodlit" by my assistant/wife, holding our godsend of a torch, so that I could see something of what I was doing. And then, having at last reached 70, Harrington Street safely, when I came to unpack the pile that was on the back seat the next morning, I completely forgot that we had left our final luxury of a duty-free bottle of Cointreau hidden among the clothing. It came out with the clothing, fell and smashed at the edge of the pavement. Margaret's father was quite sure that there would be a lot of drunken cats and dogs in the neighbourhood that day.

CHAPTER
EIGHTEEN

Early Years in Birmingham

Once back in Cleethorpes, we were soon into our normal holiday routine of lemonade lorry for me and any kind of temporary work for Margaret, whether as waitress or shop assistant. There was also the important matter of a job to be sorted out for Margaret in the Birmingham area: curiously enough, the only interview she obtained was at Brierley Hill Grammar School, just down the road from where we now live, but nothing came of that. It was not until we were actually living in Birmingham that she secured her post at City Road School, where she taught very happily for the next two terms, until she was appointed, at long last, to specialise in English at Aston Commercial School, where she really came into her own.

In the meantime, we had settled into our two rooms at Don and Doris's in Selly Park, where we shared the kitchen and the bathroom and, generally, managed to dovetail pretty well with the Gilbert family, who were very kind to us. With Don being Metalwork teacher at the same school, transport was not much of a problem for me, whereas Margaret had to take two buses through the city centre to get across to City Road, including a steep walk up to the General Post Office in Paradise Street for her second bus. We soon found our way round the centre of the city, familiarising ourselves with the very good shopping to be had in New Street and Corporation Street, and began to invest in the Birmingham Municipal Bank, from whom we would be expecting a mortgage before long.

School, for me, though full of pleasant colleagues and boys who, on the whole, were quite responsive, was somewhat disappointing because, as might be expected in a Technical School, with pupils who were there as a result of a second attempt at 13+, their interests were quite properly directed towards the scientific and practical subjects. What is more, I soon discovered what must become clear to most teachers, and not only linguists: if you take over groups whose interest in the subject has been largely eroded through previous mediocre teaching and the O Level examinations are only a short time away, then you are facing a steeply uphill struggle to reach the required standard. As previously mentioned, Bertie Brown, the Head, who had great expectations of me, had made promises at the interview which could not all be kept, both in relation to the time he would allow me with examination classes and the additional facilities he would obtain. I soon became restless and keeping my eyes open for local opportunities, was rewarded by spotting a junior French post at King Edward's Five Ways School, for which I applied. To do Bertie Brown justice, in spite of the brevity of my stay at Bordesley and despite his personal disappointment at the possibility of my hasty departure, he gave me a good enough reference to persuade Tommy Burgess at Five Ways to both interview me and give me the job, back in a good Boys' Grammar School, where I felt really at home.

When we arrived in Birmingham, our plans had already reached the stage of knowing that we would not want to live in rented accommodation any longer than was necessary. Margaret, being good with money in a way that I never was (not that I had had much opportunity!), had managed to put away a sufficient sum in her last year of teaching at Leicester so that, with a little more that came from our meagre earnings in France, we were able to start house hunting immediately. If we aimed at a house costing no more than £2,000, we would be able to find the 10% deposit which, together with a strict 2.5 times the man's income, determined the limits of one's maximum mortgage repayment. So well defined was this legal inability to take the wife's income into account in any financial arrangement that, when we selected our cooker for the kitchen, a large one that could not be paid for in a single payment, the Gas Board insisted on my signing the agreement, even though Margaret made all the arrangements and intended to pay the instalments out of her personal salary. Furthermore, so well ingrained was her mother's experience with debt and hire-purchase that there was no question about it: goods were to be fully paid for before installation, once we had a house for them to go into. This policy inevitably led to such consequences as bare floorboards while carpets were being paid off and our Dunlopillo mattress spread on the floor until such time as we could afford the divan base to go with it. There was no argument about it, because I recognised then, just as I recognise now, that I am not a good manager of personal finances and, fortunately for me, the present-day alternative of piling debt onto credit cards just did not exist to tempt me.

The two terms spent at Don and Doris's were, therefore, a period of quite intensive house hunting which, in the process, introduced us to a large sector of East Birmingham, as we followed up whatever the estate agents brought to our notice. Being in the same house as Don had tremendous advantages in relation to this for, not only had he lived in Birmingham all his life, but also, in his former capacity as a plumber, he had worked for numerous house builders around the city and he was very free with his advice as to whom to trust and in whom to have no confidence. He was also very happy to cast his eyes over any property in which we had a serious interest and knew what he was talking about, whereas we were, as are most young couples, totally inexperienced.

In the end, having looked at all sorts and worked our way round gradually from the south to the east, we settled on a house which was still being finished off by the builder on a new estate in Castle Bromwich. Don looked it over and approved: it had good amenities nearby, it was quite well placed for my school in Bordesley, (which I was about to leave, but I was unaware of it at the time), and the house itself was better than the usual three-bedroomed semi, since it had a built-in garage and the third bedroom was a good size, for it extended over the garage. Lastly and most importantly, its price was £1,900, making it absolutely right for the money we had available. Though it was not complete, the builder was able to promise that it would be ready for Easter and actually kept his promise, though his workmen stayed around in the road for some time after, making it possible for us to call on their help for the odd things which always need attention in a new house.

That Easter holiday was probably one of the most eventful of our young lives, but it started very badly, with the news that Margaret's father had had a massive heart attack and died while at work on a trawler in Grimsby harbour. When he was not working as a ship's engineer, he used his skills as a fitter to service and repair ships' engines: while down below, he had felt unwell, had struggled up on deck and had collapsed. For us, it meant immediate departure by train to Cleethorpes and doing what we could to make things easier for Mum. Those were, therefore, not only our last days with Don and Doris, but also Margaret's last at City Road and mine at Bordesley Green. It was also, and sadly, the beginning of Mum's long life as a widow though, fortunately, the fact that the house was shared by Clarice and her family meant that she was not expected to adapt to a life in isolation. Nor was there ever a serious financial problem in being left to cope on a widow's pension, since Margaret, being the daughter that she was, immediately allocated £1 a week to her mother and stuck to this arrangement for years, just in case there should be any difficulty. Mum, on the other hand, being the thrifty mother that she had always had to be, put most of those weekly £1s into a separate savings account, so that it would eventually return to Margaret in a lump.

CHAPTER
NINETEEN

New House/New Schools

We returned, naturally, well before the end of the Easter break, in order to give ourselves time to move into Windleaves Road and to go through the house from top to bottom, so that all the plaster blobs, of which there were many, would be cleaned up for when, eventually, there might be carpets in every room. Gradually, over the next year or two, the carpets and furniture, mostly ordered from Restalls in Birmingham, began to make our house the comfortable place to come home to that we had long envisaged, but always governed by the policy of not taking on any hire purchase debts. Margaret had very definite ideas about colour schemes and styles of furniture and I equally definitely approved of Margaret's ideas. Also, fortunately for me, she kept meticulous accounts of our joint earnings and put forward very sound ideas concerning where our next expenditure should be, without allowing me to fritter money away uselessly. Although in those early years equal pay for women was still more of a promise rather than an accepted fact, our joint income as young teachers was fine as a basis, but we were not satisfied to leave it at that: each of us had additional night-school classes to boost our monthly pay. Although this evening work eroded our time together, it resulted in a much speedier completion of the furnishing of the house and we were young enough and sufficiently well motivated not to resent the loss of freedom or the expenditure of energy. Indeed, the additional adult classes meant that we widened our contacts and, at times, made worthwhile friendships with members of these groups. Not satisfied with extra hours of teaching, I started as a student at the College of Commerce, where we both had classes, doing an external degree course in Economics/Government which, supplemented by a great deal of later private study, allowed me to sit the London University degree in 1958 with sufficient success to be awarded a Lower Second.

Both new schools that we returned to after Easter were a joy. Margaret was, at last, able to teach her subject to pupils who were capable of stretching her, while deriving great pleasure from simply associating with boys and girls who enjoyed being with her as a personality, appreciated her offerings as a teacher and returned the warmth and interest that she brought to them. I, too, was much more in my "milieu" at Five Ways, finding the boys and the staff highly congenial: the stress on academic learning was in the air and the boys that I taught were fully prepared to accept it. Moreover, it was possible to relax and be friendly, calling the boys by their nicknames without it ever leading to the slightest loss of control. The old Five Ways building in Edgbaston, where we stayed for the next three years while the new building was being completed out at Bartley Green was, to the inexperienced eye, an inhospitable place dating back to the 19th Century, but it had the inestimable advantage of having very thick walls, which meant that, once the boys were in and the door shut, you were entirely on your own and not interfering with the classes on either side. For the teaching of oral French and for a young teacher with rather a loud voice, this was ideal, especially since the man who spent most of his day next door was the dour Second Master, whose ideas about the teaching of boys were very different indeed. Because the building was scheduled to close in three years' time, the Governors were certainly not prepared to waste valuable resources on decoration or refurbishment, but none of that mattered in the least and my classroom hummed with good, solid work and the occasional outburst of controlled laughter. The staff room was the lightest room in the building, with a huge bay window onto the busy Hagley Road outside and, in it, there was always a good-natured gathering of the staff at morning break and during the lunch hour. There was also a marvellous character called Scudder who was the School Porter, a sort of mixture of head caretaker and messenger boy, who supervised the school entrance, looked after lost property and came round the classrooms with messages which the Headmaster wished to be "broadcast". At the rear of the building, with the old Children's Hospital beyond,

144

there was a large, asphalted yard with a wide gate to allow staff cars to enter and be parked at the far end, while the end nearer the school building was the boys' play area during their breaks: this hosted the most amazing criss-cross of games, where the boys involved were the only ones who knew which game involved whom. Over the years, the area had been gradually encroached upon by various "temporary" buildings, such as the Biology laboratory and the Woodwork hut, which also played host to the Scout troop, but none of this deprived the boys of their complicated and energetic games. For their organised sport, the boys were transported by year groups to the fields two or three miles away, where the PE staff, with the help of most younger colleagues, whether or not experienced in rugby (and, in my case, definitely not!) would supervise the afternoon's activities.

It was in that same school yard that our poor old Hillman Minx finally gave up the ghost, almost exactly three years after I first took charge of it in Leicester. Nothing that I tried — and with the old type car engine I was not exactly hopeless — or, for that matter, that the AA men tried, was able to get even a splutter out of it so that, in the end, I settled for an AA man who was prepared to tow me back to Castle Bromwich, where it resided on my home-made drive until such time as the scrapyard came and removed it, leaving me with £25 which, in those days was the scrap value of a dead car. In its place, Don Gilbert was delighted to help me find a Sunbeam-Talbot 80, the make of car that he had been converted to: it was black and sleek and sporty-looking, very eye-catching to the boys at school, with whom it raised my status to great heights! We remained good friends with Don and Doris for the rest of our time in Birmingham and they frequently came to our new house. If, as often happened, Don found me attempting a bit of DIY, he would always prefer to take it out of my hands, rather than see me struggling: it was he who taught me how to be rather quicker when wallpapering. He was also never happier than when wielding a big hammer, as when we adapted the space between the kitchen and the rear of the garage to make a laundry area.

The Headmaster of KE Five Ways was a delightful man who had taught Classics at King Edward's High School (where David was destined to go). Not only had he shown great faith in me at the time of my appointment, but he had also firmly approved of my style of teaching when he came to observe me in my first term — when I was completing my probationary year. He was not very happy about the modern language teaching in the school, especially the German, which had been the main language, and he hoped that this young and vigorous injection into French, which he was now substituting as first foreign language, would help to transform the picture. He encouraged me to think about taking a group to France in the following summer and gave me his full backing when I decided to aim for Biarritz. Gathering a group ranging from the 12s to the 15s was quite easy because nobody had offered this kind of school party before: so I soon had the 35 boys that I was aiming for, but finding other

146

members of staff to go along was rather more difficult and I nearly despaired. In the end, help arrived from an unexpected quarter: Lancashire! Margaret's father had befriended Ozzie — his surname was Osmond — when he had come to Grimsby to install some machinery at Pop's workplace and had immediately brought him home as a lodger. Ozzie had quickly made himself popular with all the family and, after hearing me mention my difficulties, had offered himself and his wife Edna as accompanying adults. His offer was gratefully and speedily accepted, as was that of Olwen Plant, the mother of one of my second formers, who subsequently became a lifelong friend.

Although the trip had much about it that was happy fun and memorable incident, like the evening at the Bayonne Festival, when Edna had handfuls of confetti stuffed down the front of her blouse and then called the perpetrator, "Eeh, you cheeky monkey!" in broad Lancashire tones, it was completely overshadowed by the tragic death of John Pritchett in the sea, on the very first day. John was a handsome 14-year-old who, although he was capable of rudimentary swimming, panicked when he found himself floundering: even though he was with a friend who tried to help him and despite the lifeguards reaching him within a minute or two, John's heart just gave up and could not be revived. I had been to the bank to sort out the group's pocket money, leaving the other four adults to supervise, and Margaret had just given instructions for all the boys to be rounded up and brought out of the water, but a small group of third formers had not heard. To describe the effect that this mishap had on Margaret and me is beyond my wit, but it was the unanimous wish of the party to stay and carry on, which is what we did. If we had given in to our — i.e. Margaret's and my — feelings and returned home then, I am convinced that we would never have taken another school party. Thus, on the one hand, it was one of the hardest things I have ever had to do when I met Ben Pritchett off the plane and then helped him to make the arrangement for John to be transported back to Birmingham in a lead-lined coffin but, on the other, it resulted in cementing a great bond of friendship with many in that group. Even more than with the boys, it established a deep and long-lasting friendship with Olwen and Wilf Plant, with Harold and May Newman and, more amazingly, with Ben and Milly Pritchett, all of whom mothered and fathered us for the rest of their lives and played such an important part in our later years.

When we arrived back in Birmingham, we were met not only by the Headmaster, who showed his support by being there, but also by many of the parents, who went out of their way to thank us and to show their sympathy — the boys had played their part by writing home and making it clear that, in spite of the sadness that we all felt, it had been a remarkable holiday. May Newman immediately took Margaret and me in hand, sent Chris off to make his own way home by bus and bundled us into her car to take us back to Castle Bromwich: that was our first encounter with that formidable lady.

Later that year, other parents of the boys that had been with us were most insistent that we should go abroad again and that they would entrust their children to us. The result was that, in spite of our own serious misgivings, but with the blessing of Tommy Burgess, we assembled a large group to go to Annecy, in the foothills of the Alps. For this tour, not only Olwen Plant, but Harold and May Newman came with us as the accompanying adults and many of the boys were those who had been in the group going to Biarritz the year before. Annecy, too, was good fun for those who came and the life in a French school, sleeping in open dormitories and then enjoying days in the fresh air, resulted in a great holiday for all concerned. What it did not do was to make demands on the boys' knowledge of the French language unless they made a great personal effort to speak. The long train journeys, however, were tedious and left a lot to be desired, giving me the impetus to think in terms of using the newly-emerged minibuses as a means of taking smaller, more compact groups across the Channel.

In the intervening years since 1954 — we were now in 1958 — the ferries had also evolved into the modern roll-on roll-off ships, which made the crossings much less cumbersome. The supportive Harold and May were quite prepared to drive a No. 2 bus, thus allowing for groups of 20 boys — not quite accurate, since Bobbie Newman had to be included — heading, this time, for La Baule in Southern Brittany. The minibus holiday became an annual event for us, continuing into my time at Leicester University, where I was able to

149

hire the Student Union buses. Imagine the panic one summer (by this time, it was boys and girls from Margaret's school at Hodge Hill who were coming with us) when, because the booked Union bus was withdrawn at short notice, we were obliged to "buy" a minibus on a sale or return basis, the garage undertaking to buy the vehicle back at an agreed price, as long as it came back in the same condition that it went out. This arrangement had a magical effect on the group's attitude to keeping the vehicle clean and untainted!

While the above activities were developing, I had enjoyed a fulfilling 5+ years at Five Ways, proving to myself and to the satisfaction of my Headmaster that, given bright pupils, examination success could be achieved in less time than the standard O Level course and that a good and determined oral-based approach was more successful in implanting the language as something to be used than the textbook on its own. Although the number of boys going through to take A Level French was understandably small by comparison with the Sciences which, even then, offered the prospect of much greater rewards, the 6th Form work was also very rewarding and even allowed me, in the case of Terry Keefe, to recommend one candidate to Professor Sykes, who succeeded in bringing the best out of him: Terry later ran the French Department at Leicester and moved on to a professorship at Lancaster.

However pleasant my teaching life at Five Ways might have been, and there is no doubt that it was — the boys were good, the staff were a happy crowd with whom I got on well, the Head made it very clear that he had great confidence in me — I was now 30 and ready for a change. I had successfully completed the degree in Economics with London External, the Open University of that time, and I was looking for a stepping stone towards the Headship that I saw myself destined for. That was when I saw and applied for the lectureship in Modern Language Teaching at Leicester University, still close to my heart from my student days only seven years earlier. I am sure that it helped that Professor Tibble was still in charge of the School of Education and that Professor Sykes was also on the panel that interviewed me. Probably equally important, since emphasis was always placed on research as well as successful teaching, was the evidence that I had, in the seven years since leaving Leicester, completed my Licence in France, added my BSc(Econ) and also gone on to do the research into careers advice in schools, aided by the generous Harrison-Barrow travelling scholarship. This was a fund set up by a prominent Birmingham City councillor with a special interest in schools and teachers, which not only gave me a sum of money adequate to finance a trip to the USA, but also maintained my teaching salary in my absence and even allowed my school to pay a temporary replacement while I was away.

I must digress, therefore, and tell you about this half term in America, before I go on with my move to Leicester University. Once I was sure of the Harrison-Barrow, Margaret also obtained leave of absence for September/October, 1959, and, in late

151

August, therefore, with a cabin trunk full of our belongings, we set sail on the *Britannic*, leaving Southampton for New York. That, in itself, was a wonderful novelty and a romantic start to what was a marvellous working holiday. Cousin Jack and his wife Rose had kindly offered to take us in for the whole time that we planned to be there — taking a great risk on good relationships, since we only knew each other by correspondence apart from my day with Jack in Paris — and it only remained for me to complete the study arrangements which I had put forward as my justification for the award. I had already written to a number of schools in New Jersey who were very willing for me to come and see how careers guidance was dealt with in American High Schools, where the provision for settling students into post-school employment had been recognised as a need for many years.

In the England of the 1950s, though I am sure that there were schools that helped their pupils with employment opportunities, very little had happened on a systematic basis and none of the schools that I was familiar with made it their concern. Birmingham Education Authority happened to be one of the few where they actually had a Careers Service that went into schools to advise young people on the employment opportunities in the world beyond school, but this had only happened with the raising of the school-leaving age to 15. By sheer coincidence, our next door neighbour in Windleaves Road was one of their advisers, giving me an insight into what was actually being done and making it clear that, with the service being in its infancy, there was ample scope for a study of the type I proposed.

We really enjoyed the transatlantic crossing, our first taste of life on board ship, and we made the most of it — dancing every evening, lounging on deck in the sunshine, making new friends and tasting the varied food. Margaret had invested in a beautiful Chanel evening dress called Mirabelle, which was absolutely stunning and would never be equalled by anything that came later: we felt as though we had made it into "High Society" but, unfortunately, our stay in the USA gave her no further opportunities for that sort of outfit and it stayed in the trunk until our return crossing.

Jack and Rose went out of their way to make us comfortable in their typically American bungalow in Westfield and also introduced us to their summer retreat at Beach Haven, where they rented an apartment right on the beach and soaked up the sun. As a treat for us, they also took a few days' leave to drive north through New Hampshire and Vermont to meet the cousins in Montreal, where several of the Mullers had settled. Robert, the eldest, had returned from the war, bringing with him the know-how which allowed him to set up in the manufacture of rattan furniture. He was joined by Joe, who had been so kind to me in London soon after my arrival, but had then been interned as an alien. Their youngest sister, Cilka, had also managed to find her way to Montreal, where she worked for the boss of an import/export business, later to be joined by sister Hella and Ferda, who abandoned their bakery in Israel to take their children

Karen and Eldad to Canada for their University education.

The social and family side of our stay in the USA was further broadened by bringing us into touch with Jack's brother Lolek, married to Sadie, and his daughter Janet and her husband Jerry. Lolek had survived the war in spite of being dragged off to concentration camp and had saved Janet by placing her in the care of some Roman Catholic nuns. Being a qualified dentist, Lolek had drilled his own teeth to be able to insert family diamonds into them, which he was later forced to use to pay for necessities — in one case, buying a loaf from a German officer by paying with a 2-carat diamond. We also spent an entire week in Dover, NJ, with Maria, Aunt Paula Laufer's elder daughter, whom I had last met in Nizna when she came on a visit to her uncle there. Earlier, also, Jack and Rose had taken us for a brief visit to Lexington, where Maria's younger sister, Helen, who was married to a delightful Chinese, Johnny, lived. Johnny was an aerospace engineer and the reason for their later moving to the San Francisco area, where we caught up with them at the end of our Helen's year in Wisconsin. However, in Lexington, we were treated to an all-American history tour by Ricky, their then ten year-old son, all geared up as a "minuteman".

All of the above makes it sound as though getting to know the family was the main outcome of our eight-week stay in New Jersey and there can be no doubt that, as it turned out, those contacts had an enormous impact on our later life because, although we continued to live at such a remove in our little world of Castle Bromwich and the later homes, the knowledge that I had a caring family overseas who all kept in touch over the years meant a great deal to both Margaret and me, who were regarded as the children of that generation. From this same visit also sprang our contact with Israel, later with Australia and, more immediately with Edith, her sister Ann and their families in London, who were so kind to us, especially in our remaining child-free years.

However, let me return to my genuinely serious purpose in going which, as outlined above, took me into a large number of High Schools in the New York and New Jersey area and gave me a broad insight into the normal running of the secondary system in general and the careers advice provision in particular. As frequently happens, the more that I saw of the set-up, the more clearly I was able to grasp how the fundamental differences in approach between the American and the English systems made much of what was done there totally inapplicable and untransferable. On the other hand, it also clarified for me how, in an English school, much more guidance could be provided without it losing its Anglo-Saxon characteristics. Not only did our stay provide me with ample material for the report which I wrote for the Harrison-Barrow Foundation which had treated me so generously, but it also created one more very useful string to add to my bow when it came, less than a year later, to providing evidence of my being interested in educational research as well as in the pure teaching of languages. As things turned out later, it became more and more obvious to me, if not to others, that my interests did not lie in the direction of research and that I did not possess the necessary self-discipline to pin myself down to writing a certain number of closely argued pages every day. Instead, I was eager to be given the opportunity of trying out some of my ideas in a school where I was unambiguously in charge and able to make decisions about such things as choice of subjects and careers information.

The life of a University lecturer did, of course, have its appeal: it was intellectually stimulating, relaxed, for much of the time, and it brought me into contact with a lot of pleasant people, both among my colleagues and also the students who were my responsibility. Furthermore, it gave me the opportunity of working inside the schools in Leicestershire and neighbouring counties where I placed my students for the term's teaching practice and some, in the city and county, where I regularly took groups for demonstration classes given by me or by hand-picked teachers of whose methods I approved. Terms 1 and 3 were college based and required a contribution to the History, Psychology and Methodology courses, whereas Term 2 was where we all got down to the work in the classroom. Here, it was my role mostly to sit at the back and give help through a critical appraisal of what I had seen when the student attempted to put into practice what we had previously discussed.

Continuing to live in Castle Bromwich and thus allowing Margaret to continue her teaching at Hodge

Hill was not at all a problem: I enjoyed driving and the roads in the early 1960s were not nearly as crowded as they have since become. It was possible to forecast reasonably exactly what time one would arrive in relation to the time one was able to set off.

This was the time of our Minis — out went the Sunbeam-Talbot, with its relatively higher fuel consumption and tyre costs, quickly followed by the little Fiat 600, which had been bought for Margaret when she was about to pass her driving test, but which had proved a bodywork disaster. The Mini had just gone into mass-production in 1959 and we were introduced to it by Sidney from London, who brought his wife, Edith and daughter Jackie to visit one weekend and gave us our first ride in this revolutionary car. Edith, too, was a Stiller, from Vienna, whom we had heard about from the Mullers while in New York and about whom I must say some warm words later. We were most impressed by Sidney's Mini and soon asked him to supply us with one through his garages in London. It was in our first, red Mini that we drove through France and Germany to Czechoslovakia, where the car was a star attraction to the natives, most of whom had never seen one before and were astonished at its space and front-wheel drive: we were definitely at the centre of attention there. It was in a later Mini also that we took our first winter skiing holiday, when we piled in with Sonia and David Burns (Sonia was a colleague of Margaret's at Hodge Hill) to go to Switzerland and enjoy some winter sunshine. Soon, we had a Mini each and, because of the heavy mileage that I was doing between home and work, the colours changed almost annually, but the Minis went on: first red, then yellow and green, then back to red again for the station-wagon version when we settled in Lancashire with a baby to carry in the back. Jumping ahead, the estate cars grew larger as our family increased in size: the Minis gave way to a Hillman or two, followed by the large Triumph, which eventually gave way to the Peugeot seven seater, with plenty of room for all the children to argue about who should sit where.

Before I leave the subject of Birmingham, I must return to the lasting friendships that we made as a result of that first tragic school party to Biarritz, when Olwen Plant had come along as a parent and had been there so fortunately to look after John, her son, when a pillow fight caused him to have a severe asthma attack. Olwen and Wilf not only took us into their family by often inviting us to go for a weekend meal, but also opened up to us their social life by inviting us as guests to the Yorkshire Society and to Masonic Ladies' Evenings — the kind of social events that, without them, we would have had little opportunity to engage in. It was very similar with Harold and May Newman — Harold was also a mason — but, although there was an equally warm, if not warmer, relationship between us, the friendship seemed somehow on a more family basis, especially in the way that May regarded herself as responsible for Margaret's well-being and was always available in a way which Olwen was certainly not. The third and perhaps the strangest, and yet the most wonderful, friendship, bearing in mind the circumstances which brought us together, was with Ben and Milly, the parents of John Pritchett who had died in Biarritz. As I said earlier, I had spent time with Ben in sorting out the return of the body to Birmingham and, naturally, as Ben flew off back home, Margaret and I said that we would see him once we returned. We invited Ben and Milly for a meal at Castle Bromwich and, when they arrived, they brought us a beautiful cut-glass bowl, saying that John had insisted, before he went off to Biarritz with us, that he wanted us to be bought something nice by the group. I cannot remember the detail of how we reacted at the time, but my eyes have filled again with tears as I write and think about it now: it was just such an amazing thing for bereaved parents to do!

From this first meeting, our association quickly grew into regular meals together, alternating between Castle Bromwich and Quinton and, quite frequently, in hotels and restaurants around the Midlands (this was before pub food became the norm) where Ben wanted us to try the menu. Ben, who sold shoes for a Birmingham wholesaler, knew his way around the area, having sampled many of the places in the course of his work and, though he stayed as thin as a rake, enjoyed his food as a connoisseur. He also derived another pleasure from his association with Margaret: he used to turn up with four or five boxes of shoes that he had selected, knowing her size (only a 3 at that time) and her taste in shoes. Ben would watch her carefully as she tried them on and was invariably well satisfied when she would keep 80% of them, paying the wholesale price —

Margaret has never been as well provided with good shoes as she was then!

Ben and Milly even felt comfortable enough with us to come, first, for a weekend away in Bournemouth and then for a fortnight's holiday on the Italian Riviera in our Sunbeam, relying on me for my driving and linguistic skills. If I remember rightly also, Margaret made Milly a holiday sundress for going away. The car, of course, chose that very time to have gearbox trouble just as we were approaching the Franco-Swiss border, giving me the choice between having it towed back to Mulhouse or forward, over the frontier to Basle. With hindsight, I should have chosen Switzerland, for that is where we had to go to pick up the replacement parts but, instead, I chose Mulhouse, where the garage relied on me to translate the instructions when they were putting the gearbox together again! As a result, we had an unscheduled five-day stop in Mulhouse, finding the places that were gastronomically attractive there, before moving on through Switzerland and finally coming to rest in Finale Ligure on the Mediterranean coast. However, even that worked out reasonably well and all of us returned home feeling that we had had a "different" experience.

With friendships like that, it was no wonder that the idea of leaving Birmingham was not too easy to contemplate, especially for Margaret who was beginning to see the light at the end of the tunnel as far as adoption was concerned. We had been accepted by Warwickshire Children's Department, who had insisted that not only did we need to show preparedness by having a baby's bedroom entirely fitted out with everything that a baby might need, but also that Margaret give up her full-time teaching so that, at a moment's notice, if necessary, she could become a full-time mother. It was at this stage that I began putting my energies into applying for headships and, of course, these had to be applied for wherever they might happen to come up. The result was that, while I might be excited at the prospect of an interview miles away, there was, at the same time, the trepidation at the idea that success would result in a move out of the Warwickshire area before the baby had a chance to materialise. And so it was that, against all the odds in most people's eyes, at the age of 33, the appointing committee at Nelson decided to offer me the Headship of that very pleasant mixed Grammar School, with 600 boys and girls and 37 staff in the north of Lancashire, a part of the country with which neither of us was familiar. This gave rise to Margaret's famous remark when I came home and told her that I had been successful and after she had had a very tearful night on the settee — no question of her sleeping beside me in bed that night — that, "It must be a one-eyed place!", referring to Nelson. She was in despair about the baby, and who can blame her though, fortunately for me, because I would never have been forgiven if things had turned out differently, the baby, our baby, about whom we did not find out until December, was already born and being fostered in a home in Warwick.

Thus, the next few weeks of 1963 were filled alternately with excitement at the prospect of a move and a new challenge for me, and with worry that our efforts at adoption through Warwick Children's Department would be frustrated by the move. In addition, there were excursions up to Lancashire to sort out a home to move into, and efforts to sell the house in Windleaves Road. Because houses were not moving too fast that winter, we were left requiring a bridging loan from the bank to cover the gap. However, by an incredible piece of fortunate timing, December, 1963 saw us packing up our house in Castle Bromwich, winding up all our connections with teaching in both Birmingham and Leicester, preparing to go back to Cleethorpes for Christmas *and* bringing our baby David from Warwick to our house on December 13th. "You are NOT going to collect that baby in a Mini", said May Newman, who insisted on driving us in her much more spacious car to Warwick for the great handover.

CHAPTER
TWENTY

Babies Come from Manchester

Given all the excited to-ing and fro-ing of that November and December, we had also been extraordinarily fortunate to light upon the newly-built development overlooking the lake in Foulridge which was to be our home for the next nearly seven years. With its lawn in the front, sloping gently down to the street and the lakeside beyond, with a mature sycamore in the middle of the lawn and even a balcony across the front of the house looking over the wonderful panorama of lake and hillside, we had a dream setting. Though the back garden was smallish and undeveloped, it nevertheless had a copse of mature trees stretching back from the fence, which gave it the appearance of being set in a clearing in the woods where we were at liberty to take walks or to cut through to the village. From inside the kitchen and through the French window in our own bedroom we had the full benefit of the amazing lake view, especially in the first few months, before the more expensive houses were completed on the other side of the avenue.

Nelson Grammar School was, in most ways, an ideal school in which to begin one's career as a Head for someone who, although his teaching had proved his competence and his work at Leicester had given unusual breadth of insight into the working of many such schools, had never had the actual hands-on experience of school organisation and administration. I was taking over from a Head who, I am quite sure, knew precisely what he was doing and had been fully in control of events: he was still in his prime, was moving on to a larger and more prestigious establishment in Nottingham, leaving everything neatly and tidily organised. My arrival was in mid year, with almost everything running smoothly, though there was one O Level group that needed me to step in for the rest of the year: I was very content about that, since I had always advocated that Heads should not cut themselves off from the classroom, but should find a way of maintaining practical involvement, important for the way in which the rest of the staff saw you. As it was English that I had to teach, I was able to call on the experience of my English expert at home for any difficulties I might encounter.

The Senior Mistress, Miss Boys, was a tremendous help to me because, although she was many years older, she made no problem of fitting in with this young and inexperienced new body. She knew exactly what was expected of her in her role with the girls in the school and she did not hesitate to make me understand if there was anything where I was falling short — in the nicest possible way, of course. Her opposite number on the men's side, Kay Openshaw, had never been allowed any delegated responsibility by my predecessor. Perhaps it was rather late to try, since he was well into his mid-fifties, but he did gradually accept a few of the tasks which should have been his and any friction which might have arisen was, as far as I know, able to be avoided. Thus, little by little, as I came to know the staff well enough, opportunities presented themselves for me to broaden the scope of what was being attempted. Bill Bibby and Marion Smith were well equipped to tackle the Careers Guidance and to prepare the University applications; John Crew, very underemployed in the French department, was enlisted to oversee the introduction of General Studies into the 6th Form curriculum and other very capable subject teachers were given broader scope. Parents, who had always been kept at arm's length, were invited to form a Home and School Association, whose aim it was to give support, but never interfere in the working of the school. Just a few miles away and almost on our doorstep was the wonderful facility of an outdoor Camp School, run by Ken Oldham, who was keen to offer us its use. For the older pupils this meant Field Studies allied to Geography and, for the younger ones, we arranged residential courses in orienteering and outdoor skills, in which many of the staff were only too pleased to participate. I think there was a feeling that the "new man" was letting light into the darker corners and that he was rather more approachable than the man he had replaced. This was true for the pupils as much as for the staff because, before very long, a social space was found for the 6th Form — just somewhere to congregate in the lunch hour — and also the new Head was much more visible around the building, having to be acknowledged by the pupils as they passed, looking through the classroom windows and doors and turning up at the far end of the building at unexpected moments. Not only did I eat my school lunch with the staff on a more or less daily basis — an important way of getting to know colleagues informally — but I joined in duty rotas for lunch supervision and playground duties. I even, for a year or two, played in the staff/student hockey and cricket matches, though it was not too long before I decided that I could do better by being umpire.

As a by-product of this more relaxed approach, many of the staff became friends as well as colleagues and, in some cases, very good friends. We made it a practice to invite some of the senior staff to the house in the evening, after the children had been put to bed and several of them were kind enough to invite us back, children and all, which was quite daring when one remembers that, even when it came to leaving Lancashire in 1970, David was 6, Ian 5 and Helen 4: Becky, of course, only arrived in our last year. In fact, bearing in mind that we started from scratch when we moved in 1964, we very quickly gathered a considerable circle of friends. We started well even before the move, when it turned out that Ron and Marge Gray — friends from Bordesley Green days — had moved from Castle Bromwich up to the side of Pendle, where they had rented a cottage: they were already there to welcome us and Marge and her girls were delighted to help with our new baby. The weekly baby clinic in the village allowed Margaret to meet and get friendly with other mums who had just "produced", in particular Joyce Green and Veronica, who had little boys in the same age group as David and who lived nearby. It was to Joyce Green's that Ian determined to move when he was three and fed up with living with the Austins, but he changed his mind before the day was over, when he realised that all was not as rosy at the Greens as he had imagined. The neighbours also produced some good friends once the avenue was fully occupied: Marjorie Bracewell who had a little boy, Helen Haigh up the road and Colin Hands, the Music master at school who, for a while, occupied the house next door but one. He and his wife, however, soon moved to Lincolnshire, being replaced by my Latin colleague, Bill Bibby and his wife Joan, much more reliable in their friendship. By this time, we were regularly exchanging visits and high teas with Margaret Boys, who looked after her elderly mother and, still in education, we had formed close friendships with the Cumberlands (Albert was Principal of the College), whose David was a pupil in the school and the Oldhams at the Camp School, who had two boys, older than ours but still very willing to play with them. Going up to see the Oldhams was a special treat for the children, allowing them to enjoy the countryside under the guidance of a man who was so good with children. The same can be said of Albert Cumberland, who used to take us all into the valley below their house in Halifax Road to search for

Billygoat Gruff and to show us where the trolls were hiding under the bridge.

Whether it was we that first invited the Thomas's or the other way round, I am far from sure. Alquin was the Divisional Education Officer and had been involved in my appointment, following this up with inevitably close contact over normal school business. It was his wife, Margaret, who became a particularly close friend of my Margaret and she, unfortunately, soon needed a great deal of support when her marriage failed and when her younger son, Mark, became more and more of a problem to her. Her crisis became far more tragic when, with little warning, she had a brain haemorrhage at the age of 41 and died, leaving her two boys to the care of their unreliable father, whom she had just divorced, while her bits and pieces were fought over by her predatory family. As one of her executors, I was briefly involved in this very sad business, but it happened just as we were leaving Lancashire and the distance from Dudley made closer involvement difficult. In a different way, through the school's parent/teacher association, we also became good friends with Mari and Temp Nutter, whose William was later to be Head Boy of NGS and who lived up above our village on Noyna Hill, where they kept a few goats on their smallholding, thus intriguing our boys.

Although, as was made clear earlier, there was little enthusiasm on Margaret's part for the move up to Lancashire, which she regarded, at first, as a sort of banishment, and although she did go through seriously lonely patches in our first year or two there, by the time we left in order to take up my post back in Dudley nearly seven years later, there was quite a tug at our heartstrings in coming away from our house and my school. After all, it had been much more than just my learning-period as Headmaster of a thriving institution and the formation of a happy social life outside, for, year by year, we had built up our family and left Foulridge with three more children to add to David, with whom we had arrived. For this, we owe a huge debt of gratitude to all those connected with the Manchester and District Children's Society, who allowed us to have what some people might see as a disproportionate share of the children who were available for adoption. David was such a good baby that we were lulled into thinking that we were naturally gifted parents: however, we soon realised how wrong we were when Ian arrived on the scene and gave us, especially Margaret, a taste of the night-time problems which we had never had with David. Nevertheless, he did his best to make good by being a delightful toddler. Fifteen months later, as a concession to me, when Margaret discovered that I "would quite like a girl", we collected Helen, thus emphasising for David what he knew already: babies come from Manchester, as he unhesitatingly told the little boy at his nursery who tried to convince him that babies came out of their Mummy's tummy.

In later years, Helen, who was what you might call "petite", if not tiny, was probably the healthiest of our children — a look at her daughter, Amelie, in her pre-school years gives a pretty good idea — but that was certainly not the case when she was one or two. She was constantly plagued by chesty coughs and flu-like symptoms and the doctor was frequently being called out to her: our doctor in Colne, though very willing, was certainly not distinguished for his diagnostic capabilities. The result, at home, was that Margaret was very often having to hold Helen upright for long stretches through the night: so much so that, when we came to go down to London to visit our friend Margaret Garvie at Furzedown College, the doctor had given us an antibiotic powder to use in case of need. However, when the expected happened and Margaret Garvie saw the state that Helen was in, she insisted on calling the College doctor, a dour Scot, who sent us straight off to St. George's Hospital in Tooting, where he had arranged for an oxygen tent to be waiting. Very quickly, the medical staff there gave us the answer: Helen had a collapsed lung and, when this was efficiently dealt with, first by the hospital doctors and then by the paediatrician in Nelson, Helen was put to rights.

Because of these health problems with Helen, we had held off asking the Society for baby number four, but now was the time and, to our delight, when it came to the following spring, we were given the chance to complete Margaret's ideal of four before David reached his sixth birthday. Not only we, but the other children also were delighted at this new arrival in the house and, of course, it proved conclusively once again that "babies come from Manchester!" There was also another reason in this period of 1968/9 which had caused us to hesitate about baby number four: it was connected with my health, rather than Helen's. To please the boys, we had added two little half-poodle dogs to our menagerie, in the indulgent way that parents often do, to avoid making a decision between the brown one that David wanted and the black one that Ian preferred. We soon found that they made demands on both patience and health that could not be met. It was on my evening walks to exercise the dogs that I was first made aware of the angina that I was lucky to have so quickly diagnosed by Dr. Alam, a new doctor in our practice. Fortunately, when we took advice about the wisdom of adopting yet another baby, the view was that no parent could be sure about what was round the corner and we should go ahead: we did and that was the right decision. That spring also, we had commissioned Ron Gray to plan and then to build the conservatory/playroom which was an excellent provision for the growing children and allowed us to open or close the doors on where they now kept the bulk of their pile of toys. There, with underfloor heating, they were able to crawl around happily on the floor which was marked out as a city with roads and parks and buildings and gave the boys endless entertainment. The next step, of course, was a Matchbox electric kit and that leads into another story.

Enter Kurt Ziehrer, a cousin from Ostrava, who had somehow traced my whereabouts (which we thought was much to his credit) and rang up out of the blue. He had survived the war, using his not inconsiderable wits and had reached Hungary where, among other attainments, he had made the national water polo team, winning a gold medal in the 1956 Olympics. He then, after the Hungarian uprising, found his way to London, made a good living in the import/export trade and was living in Greenford with his partner, a lady who was an international bridge player and his eight year old son, Robert. After meeting them in London, we made the mistake of inviting them to spend a few days with us at Christmas: a Christmas so cold and wintry that, on a refreshing and sunny walk on the moors, our fingers were nearly frozen off!

Kurt had arrived with an ample supply of whisky, knowing that we were not whisky drinkers — Margaret, because of her temperance history, I, because of the glass of brandy I consumed at the age of 14. Ian, however, was keen to taste what was in the glass and further distinguished himself by giving Kurt an almighty kick in the shin when we were out walking, having seen Kurt slapping me on the back, which he interpreted as an attack — "Don't you hit my Daddy!" It was young Robert, however, who was the fly in the ointment. Being that little bit older than our boys and being very used to having things all his own way, he wanted to dominate the playroom activities and completely took over the new track which had been David's Christmas present. In short, the visit was a complete flop and was never repeated in either direction, perhaps mainly because Kurt and his lady found us to be much too tame for their tastes.

This was the time when the abolition of the 11+ examination really began to take hold and many education authorities, including Lancashire, were seriously considering how to reorganise. Lancashire, being divided up into a number of divisions, did not settle for one type of reorganisation, but left it up to each division to propose a scheme that seemed best suited to the schools within its territory. Our division, which covered Nelson and Colne, had three selective schools within it and the College of Further Education where our friend Albert Cumberland had been Principal, but had since been promoted to a much larger College in Reading. What now became the view of our Education Authority was that the three schools should be beheaded and their 6th Forms transferred to the College, where the newly-established Principal was an aggressively ambitious man. I doubted very much whether I would be happy fitting in as his No. 2, or even No. 3, nor was I prepared to contemplate staying on in the decapitated school. Since I was still only 41 and now had nearly seven years of good experience as a Head under my belt, I was quite confident that it would not be long before I obtained a more satisfactory appointment than Nelson could now offer. And so it proved for, within a matter of weeks, I was twice interviewed for posts which promised 6th Form Colleges and Dudley, which was offered to me, even had a Headmaster's house to go with it. Indeed, a return to the Midlands not only seemed attractive because of the post itself, but it was very close to our familiar territory in Birmingham, thus enabling me to fulfil the promise I had made to Margaret ("Just give me seven years. No longer, I promise!") when we first moved up north. Dudley Grammar School, a long-established boys' school of about the same size as Nelson, had a very good reputation in its locality and the scheme for its reorganisation into a 6th Form College certainly looked promising though, of course, it later turned sour, but we were not to know that.

CHAPTER
TWENTY-ONE

Dudley, the Climax

At the time of the interview, I had had no more than a brief glimpse of the house that went with the job and I was apprehensive about Margaret's reaction when she came with me to have a look. To my surprise and pleasure, she spotted that it had considerable potential as a family home and was not unhappy about moving in, which was all to the good, since our house in Foulridge was not proving easy to sell — property in the area was seriously affected by the recent closure of a large part of the Rolls-Royce factory in Barnoldswick, just down the road. All the more fortunate, therefore, that in Dudley we had a large house available rent free, enabling us to continue paying the mortgage on Alma Avenue. Curiously enough, just as Ron and Marge Gray had moved to Pendle at the time of my appointment to Nelson, so we discovered that Margaret's school friend from Cleethorpes, Liz Boyers, now married to the Rev. Peter Hale, had moved to St. James's Church in Dudley, just up the road from where we would be living. Thanks to Liz, we were greatly helped by Michael and Hazel Flowers who lived just across the road when, eventually, we moved in at the end of August and were waiting for our furniture to arrive. First, we had a massive blowout in the fuse box and then, the next day, we were sitting down to a meal in our improvised dining room, when the heavy door came off its hinges and practically squashed poor David who was sitting directly in its path: fortunately, the door was intercepted in its fall by a packing case which had been used in the move. It did not require many days of living in the house for us to realise exactly how much work would have to be done to bring it up to the standard of safety and convenience that modern family living required. A tour of the house with my new Chairman and Director of Education, neither of whom had ever set foot in it, was sufficient to persuade them that drastic alterations were needed and quickly. There followed a period of building adaptation and reconstruction which was totally unprecedented in our lives and which, I am delighted to say, will never be repeated. Poor Margaret, with Becky still only 18 months old and, being a late walker, still crawling around, was stuck in the midst of this, while I and the older children were able to escape for most of the day. The kitchen area was the part that needed total demolition, putting it out of action for weeks, but the whole of the house needed rewiring and the ancient, partial central heating system, with its ornate and antique radiators had to be replaced by a more up-to-date system that warmed the whole house.

As a result, the entire house was invaded by workmen who might, for example, be found eating their lunch in our bedroom and leaving their banana skins under the floorboards which the electricians and the heating engineers would be pulling up all over.

Instead of a primitive airing cupboard with protruding and menacing nails, the bathroom was remodelled and the room behind, once the ancient gas fire had been removed, became a cosy bedroom for Becky. Out of the scullery, breakfast room and cellar entrance, one long and useful kitchen was created, leaving the cellar to be reached from the outside. Amazingly, a cloakroom and toilet were able to be substituted for a rear passage and coal house, whereas the small pantry was converted into a semi-utility area for the washing machine and drier. For our temporary kitchen, we were exiled to a sort of verandah, soon to be pulled down and bricked off, making us dependent on the school cook for our lunches, which were served in the former caretaker's flat, much against the wishes of the School Meals Supervisor.

In the meantime, and well before all this turmoil in the house had fully taken hold, we lost no time in re-establishing contact with our friends in the Birmingham area, all of whom seemed very contented to see us back within reach again. I particularly remember the first visit from Bob and Barbara Stuckey, when we set ourselves the goal of stripping off the dark panelling which covered the hall and staircase walls and which made the whole area look most gloomy. Between us, we set to with a variety of pointed implements, ripped all the panelling off and presented the Borough Surveyor with a fait accompli, bearing in mind that his examination had led to the conclusion that the hall was better left intact. The further incentive that we now had on offer was that we could all get covered in dust and then go across to the school swimming pool for a refreshing dip, particularly appealing to the children in the party! This novelty had a special appeal to those friends like Sonia and David Burns, whose children were of similar age to ours, making weekend entertaining much simpler and more rewarding for the youngsters. Older friends, like the Druckers, who saw my picture in the *Birmingham Post*, were soon in touch and happy to renew the friendship after seven years' gap. May Newman, typically bull at a gate, somehow managed to turn her car onto our front lawn, ignoring the drive down to the garage, but certainly showed her delight at our return to the Midlands: for us, it was a very happy homecoming.

Once all the work was finished, and this was not until December, 1970, the transformation was remarkable and everyone was delighted. We now had a super-size kitchen, extending 26ft from the back door to the eating area, with a large gas boiler installed into the fireplaces, capable of heating all the downstairs area of hall, lounge and dining room, the equally extensive landing with four good bedrooms on the first floor, then up to David's bedroom/playroom on the second. We also fell on our feet with the carpets for all of this, thanks to Raymond Effemey, the Vicar of Dudley's top Church. As soon as we arrived in Dudley, we had started receiving little notes through the door when we were not in, saying the Vicar had called: we thought this chap must be determined to drink our sherry, which he was. He did have the distinct advantage, however, of also being the Chaplain to the carpet industry in Kidderminster, giving him access to the many carpet manufacturers there, one of whom was able to find for us some excellent quality but reasonable contract carpeting, enabling us to cover all the floors in this huge house at a price that we could afford. So, after the ordeal of the first three months, we were now quickly and comfortably installed in a spacious house, where all the children had their own room, we had a large bedroom with an en-suite wash basin and dressing area, a dining room large enough to seat 12 round the table in comfort, a good-sized lounge and a huge working kitchen/dining area, with cloakroom attached. This was to become the sleeping quarters for Tramp, our delightful mongrel, who started out normally enough with four legs, but who soon lost one as a result of an argument with a car. Melody, our cat, whose name had been dreamed up by Becky, also slept in that area and kept an eye on the whole household from her position of superiority.

School, in the meantime, was providing me with many interesting comparisons to make with Nelson, which I had just left. The most striking and immediate of these was the location of the Head's study, separated by a hallway from the school office and from the Deputy's little room up the stairs in the "belfry", with the staff room in a separate house next door. In fact, with a totally separate Science Block and Gymnasium and most of the classrooms far away, overlooking the playing fields, the Head's quarters were excellently placed for living a semi-detached existence, if that was what he wanted. Compare that with the E-shaped building in Nelson, where the Head's room and the school office were right in the centre of school life, with the two staff rooms and the Senior Mistress on each side, the Assembly Hall directly opposite and people passing by all the time. The Head simply needed to put his nose out of the study door and he was immediately able to see and hear whatever activity was taking place in the school, then decide whether to go left towards the Woodwork room or right towards the Domestic Science, with the Science Labs, the Art room, the Library and other classrooms overhead. Only the Gym was in a separate building, with a 6th Form Centre added towards the end of my time there. It was not until I started getting to know the different parts of the building in Dudley that I fully appreciated the difference that could be imposed by the layout on the entire "feel" of the school to those working in it. Because of the proximity of the staff rooms in Nelson, I was a frequent visitor during breaks and coffee time after the school lunch: the staff expected to see me put my nose in when I wanted to talk to someone and did not consider it an intrusion. In Dudley, on the other hand, it meant a deliberate excursion across to Staff House and, once arrived upstairs, another deliberate effort to go through beyond the notice boards into the sitting area, making it feel as though I was intruding on colleagues' private conversations. At NGS also, by standing on the corridor outside my room, I could be sure that everybody had gone to their classes when the bell went, whereas in Dudley I had not the faintest idea of how quickly people moved in the Science Labs or in the Gym or even in the classrooms overlooking the playing fields. In both cases, however, one quickly uncovered the areas where particular attention had to be paid and it was certainly also true that, in both cases, the visible attention of the Head noticeably permeated the attitudes of staff and pupils alike. Looking back after many years of retirement, it still gives me a warm glow of satisfaction that, both in Nelson and in Dudley, with all their differences, I was able to gain the co-operation and, I trust, the respect of the teaching staff, the ancillaries, the caretakers and the cleaners, as well as the majority of the boys and girls and their parents. Many of them, I am glad to say, could and can be counted among our friends.

There was a notable difference, though, when it came to the caretakers and the groundsmen in Dudley. Unlike those in Nelson, Bill White, Tommy Brookes and Mr. Nicholls were felt to be part of the school and reminded me very much of Scudder at the old Five Ways building. Mr. Brookes and Mr. Nicholls, in particular, took a very proprietorial interest in our garden and did their best to make Margaret feel at home while I was in school, whereas Bill White and his wife were always very willing to babysit and help with other little odd jobs. These little perks were partly tradition, but also, I suspect, partly because of the contrast with the previous Head, Philip Rogers, whose attitude to staff had been very different. As time

progressed, of course, greater Local Authority involvement and financial stringency in the Parks Department
meant that two groundsmen were reduced to one and,
eventually, the attachment to the school ceased
altogether. Instead, we received visits from teams of
men who would descend on the school at someone
else's convenience, but not before Mr. Brookes — he of
the famous, "Keep off them bonks!" — retired and was
followed by Bill Smith, who managed to keep a foot in
both camps. The resident Assistant Caretaker, who
occupied the top flat in Staff House at the time that we
arrived, was a less pleasant man, also called Rogers, but
he, fortunately, decided to move on soon after our
arrival. He was replaced by Arthur Woodall and Janet,
who were delightful neighbours and friends, as well as
good workers. They could always be relied on for any
help needed, whether looking after pets while we were
on holiday or even, in Arthur's case, being much
involved with the allotment which Margaret took on in
Ednam Road to keep us in vegetables. Our luck still
held when Arthur and Janet decided to accept a move
to the Sutton School, which had a house to go with the
job, because we could not have wished for a better
caretaker and neighbour than Joe Hamblett and his
wife Joan, who eventually took over as caretaker herself
in the old High School building. They were as loyal
friends as those who had preceded them, not only to
us, but to the children also.

Within a few weeks of my arrival at DGS, Trevor
Whitehouse, who had been appointed as Deputy by
Philip Rogers, applied for and obtained the Headship at

Lordswood Technical School in Birmingham, making it
possible for me to appoint Wilf Clarke, the Head of
Mathematics in the school, in his place. Quite apart
from promoting a very good man who was the most
loyal and efficient Deputy for the rest of his brief life,
Wilf's appointment helped, at that early stage of my
association with them, to bring home to the staff that
my policy was — as it had always been and would
remain — to promote from within whenever the
opportunity presented itself, since one has so much
better and more reliable knowledge of those who are
already there and working in the school. Wilf,
unfortunately and very unexpectedly, died only five
years later, just as the school was changing to
comprehensive. He left a great hole to be filled and it
took all my powers of persuasion to talk Percy Chance
into filling it for his remaining two years. (One of our
most outstanding memories of Ian, who was just 10 at
the time, is on the day of Wilf's death, as Ian came in
from choir practice at church. "You must be very
quiet", he was told, "because Dad is terribly upset at
the shock of hearing about Mr. Clarke's death".
Whereupon Ian, who had just received his first pay as a
choirboy, came through to the lounge and offered me
the 10p — his total pay — in the hope that it would be
some comfort.)

Heart attacks like Wilf's were, unfortunately, much
too common at the time that the school changed to
comprehensive. Within a short space of time, we lost
not only Maurice Bridges, a delightful colleague who
ran the German Department and, at the same time,

had organised the Scout troop in the school, but also Les Marples, our Senior Modern Linguist, better remembered for looking after the Tuck Shop, a veritable institution, which Margaret then took over so that it would not disappear. Yet another fatal heart attack struck the Deputy Head of the Park Boys' School which, after two years of remaining semi-detached from us, had, together with the girls next door, to transfer lock, stock and barrel to the main buildings.

All of this was the consequence of the change in political control which had followed very soon after my arrival in Dudley, where, at the time of my appointment, I was scheduled to run a 6th Form College, but it was not to be. With the Labour group back in power in 1971, reorganisation of all the secondary schools into Comprehensives was their answer and, once our Grammar School pupils had worked their way through the school, a viable 6th Form would depend on our success with an all-ability intake, with the possible addition of senior pupils sent from other schools. What it meant for me, was that the years 1974 to 1978 were especially stressful, since the number of pupils would suddenly jump from 600 to 1400 and the teaching staff would increase from 35 to about 100, not to mention the secretarial staff, the laboratory stewards, the kitchen helpers and the cleaners. Somehow, we had to solve the problem of four schools merging into one, but on three separate geographical sites reducing to two. Furthermore, with pupil numbers deliberately reducing to about 900 in a matter of three or four years, this had to be accompanied by a tricky reduction of the teaching staff, many of whom would be anxiously looking over their shoulder, wondering how the merger was going to affect their job or their status and who was going to be doing what and where. Once the two Park schools were closed down in 1977, there was temporarily a great deal of pressure on the two main buildings in St. James's and Priory Roads, which gradually decreased as pupil numbers reduced. However, all of us, staff and pupils alike, found ourselves moving between the two buildings in all weathers and the human problems did not just evaporate away.

For the five years that Wilf had been there as Deputy, I had had no worries about the school timetable, a task that Wilf absolutely loved and did superbly well. When I appointed Percy Chance in his place, he warned me that, under no circumstances, did he feel able to take on that part of the job and so, that too, fell on my shoulders, which was only right and proper, since it placed the onus onto me to make all the decisions about who was to do what and where. Looking back at those years, I am amazed at the successful juggling that I succeeded in carrying out without any staff mutinies and with the pupils continuing, in spite of all the difficulties, to receive a good education and an enjoyable school life, as one would hope they should.

With the new intake of all-ability children, many of the teachers, especially some of the High School ladies, were faced with a situation which was totally unfamiliar to them and which was, understandably, a strain for them to handle. Not only did they have to adapt to teaching boys in their groups, but we also had a fair share of difficult children in the lower ability classes. Unlike the thinking in some of the other new Comprehensives, our staff and I were almost unanimously opposed to mixed ability teaching and I am certain that we did the right thing in maintaining setting in the core subjects, as has been shown by the education clock turning back full circle.

Within our own family, the effects of the 1975 reorganisation could scarcely have been more dramatic. Because the lower end of secondary was now to be raised to 12+, David, whose 12th birthday would not be until October, looked as though he would be obliged to repeat his last year in primary school, where he was already top of his class. Had he been that year earlier and able to move on to a Grammar School education, we would probably not have considered the King Edward's solution: however, we had the support of Mr. Finney, his Headmaster, who offered to give David some helpful coaching in preparation for the entrance examination, which David had no problem in passing. The major snag with this success was the daily travel to which David was subjected, since he had to leave home early and return fairly late, having taken two buses and travelled well over an hour in each direction. For most of the time, David made light of the travelling and truly appreciated the advantages of what King Edward's was able to offer in the way of a good secondary education. It was not long, however, before his back became quite painful and an examination of his spine revealed him to be in need of a belt to give him support, and of a flat surface to sleep on. When it came to Ian's turn the following year, Mr. Finney made the same support available, but neither he nor we, nor Ian himself, succeeded in awakening the same enthusiasm, with the result that Ian had to accept transfer to the Dudley School, where he was followed by Helen, then Becky and also by David at the 6th Form stage. By that time, we had come to feel, and David agreed when consulted, that the A Level course at King Edward's was unlikely to offer more success or better teaching than he would receive in our school, whereas he would be spared the tedious and back-straining bus travel to Edgbaston.

Thus it came about in 1980, when David went into our 6th and Becky started at the bottom, that all six members of the family were involved in school, though the following year saw Ian take advantage of a Rotary scholarship to spend the academic year in New Hampshire. This gave him a wonderful opportunity to escape from the oppressive control of Mum and Dad and to broaden his horizons, which I think that he was very happy to take advantage of, especially as the end-of-year coach tour was a splendid way of rounding off the year of freedom from parental control. This "freedom" was very evident when we went down to Heathrow to pick Ian up from his return flight: the girls were aghast when they noticed that he was sporting an earring and warned him that he would do well to remove it, "before Dad spots it!" There were one or two other legacies from his year in New Hampshire which made for dissension, such as the very torn shirt held together with a large safety pin, very dear to him because it had been given by a girl that he was rather fond of, and the notion that he had picked up from his American friends that parents were somehow under an obligation to provide each seventeen-year-old with a car, as soon as he was old enough.

In the meantime, David had well and truly settled into the Dudley 6th Form, including singing the part of Bill Sykes in *Oliver* and making good use of the schools' cruise to illustrate on film his special project for the additional A Level Communication Studies examination which Margaret and Tony Yates helped him to complete in his Lower 6th year.

The year of David's transfer to us was also noteworthy for two other events: Margaret chose the summer holidays to submit to the hysterectomy which had now become a pressing need — no question, of course, of taking school time for such a personal matter! No question, either, of taking the normal length of rest after the operation. She was back there for the A and O results and she persuaded Eric Wilson, our friend and GP, that, by the beginning of term, she could cope with half-time in school.

Soon after, we were all six due to join the Dudley cruise, where Margaret and I had a supervisory role and she, not surprisingly, found the stairs down to the girls' dormitory just a bit of a problem. However, I am certain that a good time was had by all and, of course, David succeeded in producing a highly innovative way of filming his project for the Communication Studies A

Level, which he completed in one year. The outstanding story which arose out of this family voyage, however, was the unintentional result of Becky's 11-year-old concept of a Mediterranean cruise. She came home from one of Jenny Banner's preparatory talks about the ports of call, looking extremely puzzled: "How can they possibly get that large ship up that narrow river?"

"Which river, Becky?"

"The one that passes by the school in Clyro, of course!"

"Are you sure she said Clyro, Becky? Could it have been Cairo?"

Did I remember to talk about the school's outdoor pursuit centre at Clyro, with which Becky was very familiar?

By the time that Ian came back from his year in the States, Helen had also reached the Lower 6th and had made up her mind that she would attempt A Levels and try for University, something that Margaret and I had not made any effort to push, knowing that, if we did, Helen would be more than likely to resist. As a result, Helen and Ian started their 6th Form courses together and, at the same time, David, with excellent A Level results, went off to Leicester on his chosen course of Law with French. The year was further enhanced by the arrival of Wallace, the son of a farming family in Vermont, who was a delightful return for the Rotary hospitality which Ian had enjoyed the previous year. I complicated matters while Wallace was with us by having a heart attack in the November, thus adding to the numerous strains which Margaret had to endure. I was again fortunate, in that I pulled through in no worse a condition than when I went in and I was able to resume work before the end of term, having booked a cruise in the Caribbean for the two of us and Becky in the Easter holidays, while the three older ones went off to France on various courses or, in David's case, some work experience arranged by our Rotary friends in Brest. Wallace, in the meantime, had much endeared himself to Margaret and me by the way that he had slotted into the family, to such an extent that he even brought our Tramp to the window of my hospital ward to "speak" to me!

With David progressing happily at Leicester, able to reside in Hall for his first year, the house was just as full with our three plus Wallace to make up the numbers, for, although the original intention was for him to be there only for the Autumn Term, he returned in the summer, when something went astray in the forecast arrangements after he had spent the Spring Term with Mr. Evers, an elderly solicitor in Stourbridge. Ian was beginning to feel his way towards a course in Politics (no guidance needed!), if all went well for him, whereas Helen, much more uncertain in her aims, had not yet come to any definite conclusion about where she was heading, though English was her strongest subject. Becky, by this time, was progressing steadily into the Middle School and had a good circle of friends: she never saw herself as 6th Form and University material — quite rightly, in my opinion, not because she lacked the ability, but because she needed the motivation

190

which was later to be provided by her practical involvement in nursing and midwifery. In return for Wallace's stay with us, his family were kind enough to host Helen for two weeks in the summer, after which she returned to be ferried across to France to act as "au pair" in a doctor's family, an episode in Helen's life which is a chapter on its own! We suspect that her brief stay in Vermont may well have been the motive behind her then choosing to combine American Studies with English Literature at Swansea — a fateful decision, as it later proved to be. Ian, in the meantime, was involved over in Brest cleaning up an over-grown river bed, in a joint operation between Dudley and Brest young people: the sort of activity that one envisages as an ideal way of bringing young people together as an educational venture.

By the summer of 1984, therefore, the family was undergoing momentous changes which were to have serious consequences for Margaret, in that the conjuncture of the three older children going off to University, my own progressive deterioration in health and her full retirement from school left her feeling not just low and dispirited, but positively depressed. Her giving up smoking in the previous February, after 30 years of the habit, probably played a part in this depression as well. Although the reasoning behind her retirement was principally that she wanted to be totally free to look after me when she saw me going from bad to worse, with no prospect of improvement resulting from the vague medical supervision I was receiving in Dudley, there was something else. Margaret had

191

accidentally overheard some most unfortunate remarks made by two of our women colleagues, relating to a senior post in the school, which was being advertised: the suggestion was that the job specification was deliberately framed by me in such a way that it would lead to her appointment. This, I think, was the last straw, even though she knew that there was not a grain of truth in that tittle-tattle, especially as she also knew that I had quite another of our female colleagues lined up for the post.

David, by this time, was going to spend his third year of study in France, at the University of Strasbourg, and having serious doubts about the law as a lifetime career. Ian was on the political trail in Colchester and was in no doubt about his main interests, though, as was later confirmed by his tutors, however correct his choice of course, he had not yet discovered the self-motivation that would produce consistent hard work. Helen, too, was thoroughly contented with her life at Swansea where, having been accepted for the Combined Honours course of her choice, she had become part of a tightly-knit circle of friends in Hall who enjoyed each other's company and intellectual stimulation. This left only Becky at home and completing her last year at school — quite fortunate, in that we were able to give her rather more of our attention than she would otherwise have had. As the year progressed, she became more and more convinced that her own future would be better served by not trying to follow the other three along the path of 6th Form and Higher Education, but to head for a more practical training which did not lead directly towards nursing, but nevertheless would help. With our encouragement, she was accepted for a Youth Training Scheme which, though mainly commercial, soon led her to a post in the Works Dept, at Sandwell General Hospital and, at the same time, gave her the general maturity she needed for acceptance on a nursing course.

While all this was going on with the children, my own process of decline was coming to a head. Just before Christmas, 1984, Margaret and I walked into Dudley to shop on the market, but split up at the Saracen's Head, leaving me to pay the papers, while Margaret walked first to the Building Society (more of a climb than I could manage) then on to the Market Place, where I would find her. What happened next was that I collapsed, before even reaching the paper shop and, after receiving mouth-to-mouth resuscitation from an unknown lady, was taken off by ambulance to hospital, where Margaret eventually caught up with me. For her, that had meant a very worrying period of waiting on the market, then following the trail back to the paper shop, where she was told vaguely that a man had been carted off by ambulance. This caused her to rush back down St. James's Road, meeting Robert, the caretaker's son, who was able to confirm that the collapsed man was indeed I. It was Joan Hamblett, his mother, who then drove her to the hospital, where I was just regaining consciousness in A&E. The cause was low blood pressure, but nobody at the hospital, not Jane Flint, the new Cardiologist there, nor Eric Wilson, my GP, nor Dr. Clark, my so-called heart specialist, was able to point out to me that two of the pills that I was regularly swallowing after breakfast were both lowering my blood pressure. It was not until the following September, in France, after my next collapse, that I was told that these two pills should not be taken together, but spaced out. As may be imagined, however, we were anxious to follow up this incident by some questions for Dr. Clark, when I had my next appointment, and I asked him whether a heart operation might be worth considering in my situation. His reply is indelibly printed on my memory: "My dear Mr. Austin, if an operation could have helped you, I would have recommended it years ago. But your left ventricle is so badly damaged that it could only make things worse". Apparently, I came out of his consulting room with an ashen face and it was not long afterwards that we came to the conclusion that the only sensible thing for me to do was to take early retirement on the grounds of ill health.

As we later discovered, again while in France, Dr. Clark, whose method of keeping a check on my angina was to make me waltz up and down a three-step, library-type stepladder, had no possibility of making a reasonable diagnosis: all he had available to him were my ECG results! What was needed was an angiogram and a test involving radioisotopes which shows the functioning of the heart muscle on a screen, both of which were quickly carried out by Rob Watson in Birmingham, after we were referred to him by John Evans, the Welshman we saw in Paris. What is more, the really annoying thing about all that, but we did not have any way of knowing it until after the series of events described above, was that Dr. Clark was not a cardiologist at all, but a chest specialist and that it was open to him, at any time, to have referred me to Dudley Road in Birmingham, where they were far better equipped than in Dudley and where I would have seen Dr. Singh or Dr. Watson much earlier. Also, had he accepted his limitations and referred me at an earlier stage, instead of retiring early, as I did, I might well have been able to go through the run-up to the operation while still working and then gone back after a period of convalescence. As might be expected, there was no reply from Dr. Clark to the letter I sent him after these events, which had proved him so conclusively wrong in his diagnosis.

Coinciding with all this, Becky also finished her schooling in the summer of 1985, leaving the three of us free to go to Vigneux in September, thinking that it might be my last opportunity to visit Daniel and Yolande. It was then that the honey and vinegar, the "wonder cure" that Margaret prescribed for me, brought about the dramatic collapse which led to the wonderful denouement already described above. Vincent, their No. 3 child, who was just 10 at that time, simply could not believe that anyone in their right mind would drink vinegar and asked if he could watch me drinking this astonishing beverage. As he watched me swallow the mixture, he could see me changing to a deathly white and then collapse in a repeat of what had happened outside the Saracen's Head. Although Daniel was not there himself to apply his medical skills, there

195

was a locum in the surgery next door and he immediately sent for an ambulance which rushed me off to the Clinique in nearby Villeneuve-St. Georges, where a Jordanian cardiologist took charge of me. After listening to my medical history in great detail, he famously concluded that my medical supervision in England was sadly lacking in expertise and that no French doctor would prescribe the quantity and dosage of pills that I was taking, unless the patient was in his late seventies and had one foot in the grave. It was he that insisted that my medicaments must be spaced out to avoid the over lowering of blood pressure and suggested that, before returning to England, I should see John Evans in Paris. Two days later, Daniel, Yolande, Margaret and I all trooped along for John Evans to see me in his lunch hour, which he kindly gave up.

The idea of a Welshman practising in echo-cardiography in Central Paris was astonishing to us and, I think, to Daniel also. Be that as it may, he fully confirmed what had been said by the cardiologist at the Clinique and he was perfectly willing, had we had the time in Paris, to carry out the necessary tests. Failing that, he was able to recommend his friend Rob Watson in Birmingham, with whom he had been at Medical School in Cardiff, and he gave me a letter to take to him.

Once we were back, we wasted no time in going to see Rob and, within three or four weeks, I had been pulled in for the nuclear test, soon to be followed by the catheterisation, where a tube with a camera is inserted into the main artery in the groin and then pushed towards the heart, sending out pictures of where blockages might be located. There can be no doubt that my angiogram must have been quite impressive, for I was not allowed to leave the hospital until such time as Rob had explored the possibility of a cardiothoracic bed in all the Midlands hospitals. Three days later, I was transferred to Walsgrave Hospital in Coventry, to be taken in hand by Mr. Norton, a very experienced surgeon, who carried out the bypass operation two days later.

There is an interesting little extension to the Welsh connection with John Evans, which deserves a mention. Across the road from our house in St. James's Road, we had become quite friendly with Ivor and Joan Howells, he being the minister at the little Unitarian church round the corner in Trinity Road. When we returned from Paris, Margaret happened to bump into Joan in the street and was telling her about my adventures while visiting Daniel and Yolande. Quite naturally, she went on to talk about our surprise in finding a Welshman practising cardiology in Paris and how kind he had been to me, to which Joan responded by saying that Ivor had a nephew working as a cardiologist in Paris. His name? John Evans, of course! One of life's delightful coincidences.

Fortunately for Margaret, I did not have to stay in Walsgrave for too many days, for traipsing over to Coventry on a daily basis can have been no joke for her. What made it easier, however, was that many of our friends volunteered to drive her over while, on the actual night of the operation, Margaret and Ian were allowed some improvised accommodation in the hospital itself, so that Margaret was able to be present in the early hours of the next morning when I awoke from the anaesthetic, surrounded by plastic tubes which seemed to emerge from every orifice in my body! I must have been a real sight! Though I remember little of my regaining consciousness, I am assured that, when I was told by the nurse that my wife was there to see me, I came out with, "Ho-ho!", which sounds reasonably lively for the circumstances. Considering that my ribcage had been sawn open for the heart surgery, I quickly felt well and on the mend but, to make sure I did not get overconfident too soon, nurses and doctors assured me that, on the third day, I would feel as though a steamroller had crushed my chest — it never happened.

Four post-operative days later, I was allowed to walk down to the entrance under my own steam, to be picked up by an ambulance which drove me back to Dudley Road in Birmingham. Here, I was once again in the care of Rob Watson and, instead of the calm of the small divided wards at Walsgrave, back in the older, traditional Nightingale wards which have some very notable pluses and minuses: there are 26 beds to be seen, so that there is always something going on and no chance of being bored but, as opposed to that, there is no escape from those people or activities that one might well wish to be without. In my case, I hated being only a few yards away from the Day Room, which exuded clouds of stinking cigarette smoke every time the door was opened and I was even more opposed to the man in the bed opposite, who had been put in charge of the ward radio and who felt it to be his sacred duty to switch it on at full volume every morning at 6.30. My exasperation with some aspects of the ward organisation and the lack of consistency between the numerous ward sisters and the way they expected things to be done was such that I poured all my frustrated headmasterly feelings into a critique which ran to several sides of A4. It must have reached somebody in authority, because Rob Watson knew about it, but whether or not it resulted in any beneficial change for those who came after me must be a matter of considerable doubt. It was at least 15 years before my prayer for the return of hospital matrons was answered, but that was one very desirable outcome and, later, the introduction of a "no smoking" policy was another.

In spite of all that, City Hospital, as it was renamed several years later, and Dr. Watson earned my very sincere thanks and long-term attachment, as evidenced by our (both Margaret's and my) very full participation in the committee which was first attached to the British Heart Foundation and then, later, the Hearts of England Association, which I chaired from 1993 until 2003. It was through the HOEA that we became friendly with Kate and John Cottam, who further cemented my relationship with City Hospital by starting me off on the road to a prostate operation which was performed there in 2001.

CHAPTER
TWENTY-TWO

My Worldwide Family

Returning to my heart . . . after those few days recovering in Dudley Road, I was sent home with instructions to start walking, slowly and briefly at first, then gradually extending the distance on a daily basis and, before long, I was feeling capable of returning to a normal life. Margaret, too, with a great weight lifted from her shoulders, was feeling far better and it became possible once more to think of things other than health.

We realised that, with only Becky remaining at home full-time, 16, St. James's Road was much too big for our needs and would rapidly be a drain on our reduced income. With school now a thing of the past, there was no reason to stay there and we started looking around energetically for something more suitable. The search had to be speeded up because, much to our surprise, the house in St. James's Road sold astonishingly quickly to become a Nursing Home for the Elderly. Thus, less than 12 months after my operation, we moved six miles away to Pedmore to a 1960s house with good accommodation downstairs, but smallish bedrooms and a bathroom that looked like a film star's dressing room, features that Margaret was never able to bring herself to accept. The result was that, no more than 14 months later, we moved again, this time to the house in Priory Close which Margaret felt able to adapt to her own liking — in Pedmore, she could always see the face of the previous owner, with a grin like the Cheshire cat!

In the meantime, Becky, having reached her 18th birthday, had been accepted for her nurse training, at Shrewsbury; Helen, after spending an academic year in Wisconsin, had returned to finish her degree in Swansea; David had launched his career in the Foreign Office and was soon to buy his first property in Abbey Wood. That left Ian, who had high hopes of getting on the bottom rung of a journalistic ladder in London, but was forced to come down to earth and accept that, much against his will, a return to the parental home in Dudley/Pedmore was the only sensible and manageable answer. It is not difficult to see, therefore, that my emergence from a long period of heart problems and my retirement from school ushered in months of hectic activity centred on the children, who were all beginning to find their feet. Add to that our own return to Central Dudley (Margaret hated the house in Pedmore so much that 14 months was all that she could stand), immediately followed by Helen's announcement that she and her American Andy wished to get married in early July (1988) and you will see that the word "hectic" is no exaggeration, especially as wedding preparations were accompanied by builders working in our kitchen and Ian was still at home! Before long, however, he, too, was finding his way to a career in public relations in a firm the other side of Birmingham.

On a totally different front, on behalf of the Rotary Club, I had become heavily involved in an exchange with Poland, still, at that stage, behind the Iron Curtain, and this resulted in five young executives from Warsaw coming to Dudley in the November of 1986. For their visit, I had arranged a packed programme of factory/works tours in the locality, supplemented by outings to the theatre and the newly-opened Symphony Hall in Birmingham, as well as Rotary functions where other Rotarians were able to meet them. The intention was that, even though there was no Rotary in Poland in communist times, the visit to Dudley should lead to a similar group visit to Poland, which eventually materialised two years later. When this invitation came, I involved the Club in selecting a group of four young, up-and-coming men and women, to be joined by a young Frenchman sponsored by our French "twins" in Brest. Thus, in the autumn of 1988, Margaret and I led this group on the return visit to Warsaw and Krakow. Since we were being hosted by the actual Polish team rather than by any organisation, this expedition had also to be financed by our Rotary Club, though Margaret, who was a supernumerary, was responsible for her own expenses. We, too, were taken on some interesting industrial and commercial visits and on cultural expeditions which even included rafting on white water high up in the Tatra mountains. The visit also included a day in Auschwitz, which left an indelible imprint on us all and made Margaret and me

202

determined soon to follow up with a visit to Treblinka. Our Dudley hospitality, which had included their team being hosted by Dudley Rotarians in their homes could not, in Polish circumstances, be reciprocated because of the very different conditions under which they lived, but it was certainly most warmly repaid in every other way.

While we were in Poland, Margaret and I took the opportunity to hop across to Budapest and make contact with George Heiman and his family, with whom Maria had put us in contact. Though I am still very unsure about my exact connection with the Heiman family, they must have been very close, since my mother used to entrust me to them in Nizna for most summer holidays and Annie, in particular, spent a good deal of time with me and my sisters as a sort of nanny in my early years — as witnessed by her frequent appearances in the photographs in my Czech album. Both Poland and Hungary, because of Communist rule, were, at that time, inexpensive and interesting for the visitor, this being one more reason for our return in '89 and '90.

As a result of that first visit to Poland, Margaret and I were moved by what we had been shown to be the deprivation in which many of the ordinary people lived to make a real effort on their behalf. Margaret was, at that time, devoting a lot of her energies to making dried flower arrangements and it was largely due to her energetic approach that we raised over £500, to which the Dudley Rotary Club offered a matching amount. We borrowed a van from our Rotary friend, Ray Glazzard, filled it with things that were going to be helpful and "treats" for an orphanage (towels, t-shirts, bananas), an old people's home (clothing) and a children's hospital in Warsaw (hoist for the hydrotherapy pool) and set off through Germany, arriving in Warsaw the following day. A contact of Margaret's at Central Methodist in Dudley had put us in touch with her parents, who hosted us and we were met with a great deal of kindness by them and by strangers upon whom we chanced on the journey.

As planned, also, not that we were there with our own transport, we took a day to make a pilgrimage to Treblinka, the death camp where my mother and sisters had been murdered in 1942. Unlike Auschwitz, not a single building was left standing here, no piles of spectacles, no heaps of shoes, no mountains of abandoned suitcases with the names of their owners, herded off to the gas chambers. Treblinka is a clearing in the forest, with a lone railway siding as evidence of its sinister use and a stone memorial with concentric rings of boulders which had been brought there from every town and village in Poland. Where Auschwitz affects you with the evidence of mass murder, Treblinka overwhelms you with its deathly silence: the rest is left to your imagination.

In 1990, we met Jack and Rose and Lonek and Jeannette there, in order to spend a few days visiting their home territory in Krakow, where Lonek was born, and in Nowy Targ, where both Jack and I had our roots. This was a unique opportunity to be shown around by my two senior cousins, whose memories of their youth were still crystal clear and who were both fluent Polish speakers. One of Margaret's most vivid memories of that visit was when a cheeky Pole pinched her bottom in broad daylight, as she walked along a Krakow street with Rose and Jeannette — she was none too pleased when I asked her if the Pole was drunk! Mine, on the other hand, is of the reception which Jack and I received when we visited the family house and corner shop in Nowy Targ, still known to the locals as "The Singer". We were invited upstairs to meet the present Polish proprietor and to have tea, but that did not prevent Jack from telling him, in no uncertain terms, that he had no right to be there and should hand everything back. We discovered, when we came out onto the Town Square, that Margaret and Rose had been biting their nails all the time that we were in there, in case Jack's fiery temper caused him to say something more objectionable.

For a little boy of 10 who came to England all alone and who, by reason of war, was cut off from his family, it cannot be said that I ended badly on that front. Of course, the loss of my mother and my two sisters was something that could not be compensated for and there is no means of knowing what sort of life we and the other family members would have had if Hitler and the war had not intervened. But, leaving aside the "new" family that I gathered by meeting and then marrying Margaret, as time went by and in keeping with the diaspora, I pieced together a wonderful family on my side, spread over most continents of the globe and all of them, in their own way, prepared to welcome me, my wife and my children whenever the opportunity has arisen. It really all goes back to Aunt Paula Laufer in New York, who kept in touch with me through Philip Austin all through the war, not only sending the occasional parcel of goodies (filtered through Mrs. Austin — how much reached me is difficult to guess) but also second-hand clothes, which kept me reasonably dressed in my early days as a student. There were the trousers which ripped beyond repair as Margaret sat rather too close to me early in our association, resulting in my having to wear a suit borrowed from my friend Hoppy — which brought the comment from someone: "Doesn't Fred look smart today?" Paula, who had been my mother's best friend, as well as first cousin, in their days as young women in Budapest where my mother was training as a photographer, was one of the Heiman family. She must already have been married to her very talented artist husband (whose pictures we have all shared), because Maria, their eldest daughter, was in her 30s when she came to Nizna, while I was there, in 1938 — with the result that Maria always thought of me as that nice little boy who walked with her to the station in Podbiel. And even Helen, Paula's younger daughter, who inherited her father's artistic talent, remembered visiting my mother in Ostrava in the early 1920s, when my mother bought her a pretty little glass beer tankard — now in our Helen's possession — when she threw a tantrum and her own mother would not give in to her.

I have earlier described the way in which my cousin Jack Singer survived the horrors of three years in Japanese prisoner of war camp and then managed to make his way to the USA. Whether it was passed to him in his genes, or whether his wartime experiences shaped his later character, he was certainly one of the most determined men we have ever associated with and the greatest of all survivors. His brothers, Lolek and Adek, were very different in character, though equally affectionate towards us. Adek had settled in Israel before the war and lived most of his adult life in a kibbutz, where he brought up his family. Lolek, who had trained as a dentist in Poland, somehow survived the concentration camps, though, as can be imagined, at some considerable physical cost, emerging from the camps with a weight of about 85lbs. He had managed to save his daughter Janet (Americanised) by entrusting her to some Catholic nuns, who, though she was pushed from pillar to post, managed to bring her safely through the war. They then made their way to the USA where, together with his second wife, Sadie, he set up in a hardware store in Newark.

We met them first during our stay with Jack and Rose in 1959, but kept up a steady correspondence with Sadie for more than 20 years. All the children met her during our 1979 holidays, though Lolek had, by that time, died on the operating table, when his heart operation failed to do for him what mine did for me a few years later. Sadie, very sadly, declined into Alzheimer's shortly afterwards, when her letters became totally indecipherable. Jack also put me in touch with my other first cousin, Lonek, about whom I have already written in relation to Poland in 1990: he and his wife, Jeannette, have also remained close, ever since our first journey to Israel which could easily have ended in disaster when the Comet in which we set off crashed in Ankara. Without our knowledge, our travel agent, Mr. Shutz, had arranged for us to change planes in Athens onto a direct flight to Tel Aviv, thus arriving there several hours earlier than the Comet was due and, by incredibly good fortune, taking us off the doomed plane. Let us return to Lonek, however, another emigre in the 1930s who had made his life in insurance, after coming through the war in the Jewish Brigade and salvaging his sister and brother-in-law from the post-war chaos. Very soon after our 1962 visit Lonek and Jeannette found their way to us in Castle Bromwich and, much later, came to meet our children when they were grown up and married.

From the point of view of family contact, the two-week stay in Israel was most eventful and rewarding. It must have been through Jack and then through Adek that Berta, Edit and Erno, survivors from my father's side of the family, had heard about us and started a correspondence which culminated in our stay with Berta, who shared her small flat with Ruti, her daughter, but was most willing to put us onto her living-room settee. Erno, the youngest of the three, had survived through sheer resourcefulness, whereas his two sisters had the tattooed numbers on their wrists to prove that they had survived internment in Auschwitz. Though it was not something they wished to discuss at length, Edit, in particular, was able to relate some of her experiences: I particularly remember the way we cringed when she spoke of the operation on her mastoid ear without any anaesthetic being used. She also had a funny response when Margaret confessed to having put up with psoriasis, which had also troubled Edit as a young woman — her mother, apparently, had tried everything, but without success, and it was not until she went to Auschwitz that she found the cure: life in the concentration camp made it disappear like magic, or so she claimed.

Out of the blue, also through Adek, we were literally descended upon by Fredi and Mariana. Imagine our surprise at being found by another Fredi Stiller, the son of my father's younger brother Adolf, who had taken his family eastwards through Russia to Siberia and had succeeded in keeping them all together to reach Israel after the war. Being a baker, he had few problems in making a living in an Israeli village where he and his wife Sabena had brought up Fredi and his sister Batia, one to be a well-qualified industrial chemist, while the other was a senior sister in a Haifa hospital. When we met Adolf, it was obvious that, in his younger days, he would have borne a strong resemblance to my father, as portrayed in his wartime pictures in my album, though probably a smaller version. Fredi and I, I am afraid, look very little like each other, but we had no difficulty in striking up a close friendship with him and Mariana, a little younger than we are, both making their own mark professionally: Fredi as first chemist and then manager of Carmel Winery, Mariana in the Weizmann Institute, specialising in water conservation. They already had Edna running around as a little toddler and she would soon be followed by her twin brothers Yair and Gideon. Fredi and Mariana first visited us in

Castle Bromwich and have since been to England on numerous occasions because they love London and going to the theatre, but the children will best remember the visit for the twins' Bar Mitzvah and, later, when Gideon was on a backpacking tour. In the other direction, we have stayed with them in Richon Lezion (home of the Carmel Winery) three times, the main time being for my 60th birthday in 1988, when the children clubbed together to pay my fare. Fredi's job once led to his TV appearance on the Israeli version of *What's my Line*, after which he received a telephone call from a man who wanted to know if he was the Fredi Stiller who had been at school with him in Ostrava: to which he was able to reply: "No, but I know exactly where to find him". As a result of that, I received a copy of a photograph taken of my class of 1938/9, to which I was able to put a good number of names.

As a further contact with my family in Ostrava, Fredi also put us in touch with Bela Borsky who, as a youth, had stayed with us while he was studying mining in Ostrava: he not only remembered taking me with him to football matches on the other side of the river, but also had some stories about what happened to my family after I came to England. When they were expelled from the flat in Bank Strasse, my mother and sisters had, apparently, been forced into a room which looked out onto the cemetery where my father was buried. The cemetery was surrounded by a six foot wall, on which, as tends to be a worldwide phenomenon, there would often be slogans written: one that he particularly remembered was "Juden heraus" (get rid of the Jews!), in response to which, my sister Trude, a spirited 16-year-old, had crept out in the night and had written, "Deutschen herein" (put the Germans inside the cemetery!)

I think I have already made reference to the Muller family, who lived just a long tram ride away from Ostrava in a heavily industrialised suburb called Witkowitz, where father Muller had a cork factory, whose main attraction for me lay in the view that it had, at the rear, on the ice-hockey rink. The Mullers were also related through their mother to the Singers/Stillers in Nowy Targ and regrouped after the war in the Montreal area, where Robert, returning from the far East, having been in the Phillipines at the same time as Jack, started up a rattan furniture business. He was joined by Adolf (better known as Joe), who had been in England and was then interned, first in the Isle of Man, and then in Canada. Joe had tried to keep in touch with me, but was probably blocked by the Austins, as was Cilka, who actually came to the house in Liverpool and was turned away by Mrs. Austin. Cilka was the youngest of the Mullers, remembered by me as the dental assistant in Ostrava at the dentist's who "crowned" me in my last few weeks there. The work he carried out inside my mouth has been the admiration of all the dentists who have dealt with me in England. Cilka and Margaret really took to each other when the Mullers came down to New York while we were there in 1959 and we kept up a regular correspondence with her until she died. She will also be well remembered by the girls, who stayed with her and Budd during our visit in 1979. And it was to join the family group that Hella, another Muller sister, brought her husband, Ferda, and two children, Karen and Eldad, out of Israel, stopping with us in Castle Bromwich on the way. Hella was the sort of marvellous character that cannot be forgotten and I know that David has his special memories of Ferda from the boys' stay with them in 1979. Since then, of course, they have reduced to Eldad, but he is still as warm with us as all the Mullers have been, as Helen found when we visited Burlington after her year in the USA. With Hella, we also kept up a steady correspondence and, in her case, it was mostly in German, as had also been the case with Berta, Edit and Erno: looking back on it, I am quite surprised at the amount of correspondence that Margaret and I kept up with members of the family and this, I am sure, is the main reason why we really felt linked into my worldwide, scattered group of cousins of all generations.

Curiously enough, it was Helen's wedding to Jerome which was the catalyst in bringing us together with Roe and Silv, the twin daughters of Lonek's sister whom, of course, we never met. She and her husband had emigrated to Australia a few years after the war, having first lived in Italy. How he managed it I cannot imagine, but Lonek, who had fought through the war in the Jewish Brigade, and found himself in Italy when the war finished, determined that he would find his sister and, if possible, her husband. Like most Jewish girls, his sister and their mother had been taken to a concentration camp which his sister had survived, presumably by being a useful labourer, and, together with thousands of other displaced persons, was wandering across Europe in search of a "home". For those of us who were safely in England or in some other country not as seriously touched by the general post-war displacement, it is impossible to imagine the chaos which must have reigned in the Central Europe of that period at the end of the war. Nevertheless, somehow, Lonek managed to find both his sister and her husband, leaving them reunited in Italy. As for Roe and Silv who, through Lonek, were in regular touch with Jack and, through Jack, had our address, all the credit for our contact must go to Roe, who started things off by sending Christmas cards. Then, by pure accident, in my Christmas note in 1998, I mentioned that Helen's (2nd) wedding was due to take place the following summer and issued a vague invitation for Roe and Silv to come, if they happened to be in the vicinity. To our great pleasure, they took me at my word, since our date happened to fit nicely with their plans to go to Poland that summer: not only did they come themselves, but they also extended our invitation to Wojtek, a cousin from Stockholm whom I only knew through telephone conversations, who also decided to come. Thus we all had occasion to extend my growing family and, as a result of their being guests at Helen and Jerome's wedding, we followed up with three visits to Australia in fairly quick succession, including being guests, in our turn, at Naomi's (Roe's daughter's) wedding, which was a memorable event. As one thing leads to another, we also took the opportunity of getting to know Silv and her husband, Richard, better by driving them through France and helping them on their way to the Mediterranean cruise which they had arranged.

In following up with you my family spread over the globe, I have made one glaring omission and I would be very much at fault if I passed over my Stiller cousins living right here in London. Though I mentioned Edith and her sister Ann and their kindness to Margaret and myself, that leaves unsaid the warmth with which Edith threw open her house in Wembley to the young married couple that we were just after our return from my 1959 stay in New England. Their lovely house in a quiet cul-de-sac cannot have been completed very long and was a real dream, both inside and out, where there was a beautiful and spacious, well-tended garden. Sidney, her Scottish husband, owned three garages and was astute enough to have an early grasp of the money to be made from leasing cars. Ann, on the other hand, with her husband Dave, who manufactured furniture, and her children, lived a much more sophisticated life in an elegant flat just off the Marylebone Road, near Baker Street. When we were invited there for lunch, we were completely overawed by the Louis XV furniture and the maid waiting on us at table. The discussion in the afternoon centred on what show or film John, their eldest, and Dave could go and see — but there was nothing that they had not already seen! In those early days, when Edith's mother was still alive, I am sure that we were told the family history in Vienna, but in typical young man's style, I did not take all the stories in too carefully. The important point is that, as a young couple up in provincial Birmingham, we always had a room and a bed when we wished to be in London and, for the next forty and more years there was always smoked salmon waiting for us at 25, The Drive. It was at Edith's that we met Cousin Willi, who assured Margaret that she had married into the aristocracy, for, according to him, an outpost of my family had owned a "Schloss" in Bohemia, and Maurice Stiller, also definitely related to me (though I never cross-checked this) was the one who discovered Greta Garbo and made her famous. How Edith managed it, we are unsure, but she kept up her zest for life and was the same lovely Edith until well into her 90s. Her death, last year, marked the end of an era, but we are left with the wonderful memory of the way she danced at her ninetieth birthday party (while Sidney swore blind that she hated all the attention!) and of her unbelievable energy at Helen's wedding to Jerome, when she certainly brought Wojtek to his knees. Fortunately, her daughter Jackie, whom we have known since she was a teenager, has inherited much of her mother's character and is now a wonderful grandmother. You can see, therefore, that, after the wartime and immediately post-war period of being an isolated boy with no obvious family of my own, I gradually gathered in quite a widespread but undoubtedly affectionate family of my own, who all think of Margaret also as family and who know all about our children and grandchildren.

CHAPTER
TWENTY-THREE

Loose Ends

I think it is high time now to round off this tale of a life that could have turned out very differently IF — and there are so many ifs! Who knows what would have been the outcome if my peaceful and sheltered life in Ostrava had continued uninterrupted by Herr Hitler? So, clearly, my displacement or relocation in 1939 was the single most important factor in turning Fredi Stiller, the little Czech/Jewish boy (who looks as though butter would not melt in his mouth in the attractive family photograph, taken in that fateful year) into a fairly typical English teenager of the 1940s.

Earlier in this narrative, I have made it very clear that Philip Austin, who brought me to England and oversaw my upbringing during my teenage years, was far from being an ideal father figure. Nevertheless, I would not wish to deny him my gratitude for bringing me out of Central Europe and out of danger, nor would I wish to suggest that he failed in his efforts to ensure that I grew up into an acceptable adult. He and his mother, though scarcely able to be regarded as a family of choice, certainly conveyed to me the importance of good manners and civilised behaviour, all of which was strongly reinforced by my school and by my foster-parents in St. Albans. Being in a house with three well brought-up ladies inevitably places a heavy emphasis on good manners and quiet restraint! The school, too, even though evacuated all through the war, was a civilising influence, especially, perhaps, the school Scout troop, where I learned such a lot about living harmoniously at close quarters with a wide variety of people. I cannot, therefore, speak highly enough of my debt to Hastings Grammar School, its staff and my fellow pupils, who certainly shaped the man I was to become and who did as much as any of those early influences to integrate me into English society. Strangely, though, it was not until I came to live with the Crouchers during my 6th Form years that I felt real warmth and the sort of affection which, I hope, was the norm when we had children of our own and which is still there for our children and grandchildren. Mrs. Croucher, though I came to her simply as Derek's friend, had the knack of making me feel part of her family and became for me the first real substitute mother, to be followed shortly by Mum in Cleethorpes.

One more credit needs to be given to Philip Austin — it was entirely due to his pressure that I went to Leicester after my weak showing in the HSC examination (the A Levels of that time). Going to Leicester, after the hiccup of the first year, when I was told that there was no grant for me until I became a British subject, was the real turning point which resulted in my becoming who I am. Meeting Margaret and learning so much from her about being more serious and purposeful in my approach to life, in addition to the obvious and overwhelming emotional attachment which was there, put some backbone into the hitherto lethargic and irresponsible boy that I had been. She it was who gave me a vision of our future lives together and my total acceptance by her family, when they knew so little about me, made all our plans a reality. Where my involvement with Margaret solved the emotional future for me, Leicester also brought out the best in me academically and it is impossible to overstate my debt to Professor Sykes for the challenges that he placed before me and for the confidence in my ability that he showed.

I think I have dwelt sufficiently on Margaret's ability to handle domestic accounts not to have to re-emphasize that it was thanks to her that we were able to buy our first and second cars, to become so quickly established in a home of our own, where we had all the comforts and were then able to think seriously of bringing up a young family. It was Margaret's determination which saw us through to the arrival of David, but our good fortune in falling upon the Manchester and District Child Adoption Society which meant that, in the space of six years, we were able to gather four babies and thus rectify the handicap that Margaret's "immature uterus" had placed upon us. How different our lives would have been without those babies and how great our lack of fulfilment had we been refused them! Forty years later, with ten grandchildren to brighten our lives, the thought of having gone through life without those children is hardly possible to contemplate.

Teaching in Birmingham, though it may not sound very inspiring, was yet another stroke of good fortune for me, for, all through my years at King Edward's Five Ways, I had the encouragement of Tommy Burgess, who showed complete faith in me and, when the time came to move on, gave me his full support. The same is true of Professor Tibble, once I arrived back in his School of Education at Leicester: he knew me of old, of course, having helped me over my initial grant difficulties and then again in my Diploma year. All of this confidence and backing from my "superiors" was what resulted in my progression to a headship at 34 years of age, in a profession which does not always favour youth.

The arrival of angina at the end of my period in Lancashire signalled a focussing on health problems in the 1970s: the removal of a lypoma from my forehead, a gall bladder operation and a hernia repair were accompanied and followed by a deterioration in my heart condition, leading eventually to my early retirement in 1985. My good fortune in Vigneux (at Daniel and Yolande's) in September of that year and my successful bypass operation in November must surely be seen as the major turning point in my later adult life. For me to be able to sit here, twenty-three years later, writing these lines and looking back on those years of rewarding retirement is not far short of the miraculous. Neither Margaret, nor I, nor Dr. Clark, my pretend heart specialist in Dudley, would have given much for my chances of surviving to the age of 60, let alone 80. The role of Rob Watson and of Mr. Norton in this success story has already been fully described and, having had my heart refurbished, I then followed up with prostate cancer, to be removed by Mr. Ryan — again at Dudley Road (now City) hospital, my favourite health resort! Some part of this huge debt which I owe for my good fortune, Margaret and I have worked to repay through the heart committee that was formed immediately after my operation, but I would be the first to recognise that the full debt can never be repaid.

That the last 20 years have been as satisfying and as gratifying as they have is due largely to a happy home life, supplemented by fulfilling activities outside the home. All of these, Rotary, the Baylies Trust, as well as many of our closest friendships, stem from my position in school and from contacts developed there, for, had it not been for school, I would not have been invited to join either. Maintaining my contact with the Old Boys' Association of King Edward's Five Ways was the key that gave entry to two other groups of friends in our later life: both arose as a result of going to annual dinners organised for former pupils and staff of the school. The first and, in many ways, less unexpected of the two was when we were seated close to a group of ex-pupils from the 1B, whose form master I was in 1955, my first year there. A tightly-knit group of these boys had not only gone through school together, but had, in their 6th Form years, become involved with a group of young trainee nurses from Dudley Road Hospital (as it then was), with the happy ending that

220

several found their partners for life together and had double the reasons for staying in close touch. From this group of now 60+-year-old "little boys", we managed to attract David and Margaret Reeves to join the committee of the HOEA, to which they brought their bright ideas and where they also joined Vic Lyttle, another of my ex-pupils from a different year group. As a result of this, a dozen or more of David's year became regulars at our lunches and took on the organisation of the tombola, into the running of which they threw themselves wholeheartedly. Amazingly, this group had also in their late teens, through their friendship with Chris Newman, become proteges of our dear May, who loved to be surrounded by lively young people and had also involved Bobbie, Chris's sister. This, then, is one way in which our lives have come full circle.

The other, and more unexpected way, came about after a similar dinner a few years later, which was held in the Students' Union building at Birmingham University. As we left, I stopped to read some notices, one of which advertised a French evening (with French food!) at the Synagogue in Sheepcote Street (since demolished) for a princely £10 a head. Margaret and I felt sufficiently attracted to this to make certain of our tickets on the Monday morning and duly went along out of pure curiosity. Although we were complete strangers to the people there, and I have a strong feeling that not many strangers were normally expected, we were made to feel most welcome. The meal deserves a mention, for it consisted of the weakest onion soup imaginable, followed by quiche and salad and, finally, a chocolate eclair: not difficult, therefore, to work out what was French in the French food. However, the outcome of a conversation with one of the ladies who came to see who we were and why we had come was, first and foremost, that we were introduced to Lia who, like me, had left Czechoslovakia as a child, in her case on the Kindertransport, and Philip, her husband. We were immediately invited to their house in Moseley, to which invitation we were quick to respond and, as a result, have joined the Association of Jewish Refugees in Birmingham and have met some lovely people, bringing me full circle to my early roots.

There can be no doubt, therefore, that coincidence has played a large part in our lives of late and none more so than the most recent and, perhaps, the most astonishing. Just a few months ago, at the end of March, 2008, I had been asked to be the castaway in *Desert Island Discs* at Rotary. This follows a standard format, developed over the last years, where my colleague, Mike Summerfield, interviews the chosen "victim", extracting his history and views of the world, punctuated by that same individual's choice of music to accompany his story. Not surprisingly, my tale began with my childhood and upbringing in Ostrava, which I described as a largish and grimy industrial town in Northern Moravia, on the Silesian coalfield, which supported both its mining and its iron and steel production — aspects of Ostrava which I remember well. I also described my parents' shop, run by my mother for all of my 10 years, since my father had died when I was a mere 4-month-old baby. I made a point of saying to my audience of Rotarians and their wives that I thought it most unlikely that anyone among them would even have heard of Ostrava, in its middle-European obscurity, unless, by chance, they were such football enthusiasts that they had noted its team's occasional success in the UEFA cup competition. Imagine my surprise, therefore, at the end of the evening, when I was approached by a visiting and unknown Rotarian who had been in the audience, who declared that he not only knew of Ostrava, but that he had lived and worked there for a year in the employ of the Czech government. Tom Elliott, a mining engineer and consultant, one of two from the Bewdley Club, who had quite unpredictably come to us because their own Club had decreed a "Scatter Evening", added that he would be returning to Ostrava a fortnight later for some unfinished business and would be happy to make any enquiries or take photographs on my behalf.

Even before he set off a fortnight later, Tom had e-mailed his former PA in Ostrava, giving her some details concerning me and she, in turn, had passed all of that to her mother, a lady much nearer to my generation and Jewish to boot, who, in conversation with an older friend, discovered, to my complete astonishment, that I might be the son of Ignatz and Rosa Stiller. When Tom returned, having taken some photographs and bearing all kinds of helpful information, street maps and booklets, we spent a morning together, as a result of which Margaret and I, quite independently, concluded that it was the right time for us to go back and have another look. We had, of course, gone to Ostrava together in 1962 BC (before children!), when we did a tour in our first Mini, but that visit was not tremendously productive, partly because I knew nobody living there, partly because my own attitude at that age was totally different and, dare I say it, more superficial and, partly also, because Margaret was very worried by the communist regime and what it might do to me as a former Czech national. This time was different: we had a most helpful friend and guide in Judita, who took pleasure in meeting us and showing us around both the town and its surroundings. She introduced us to the Jewish Centre where my mother and sisters were commemorated on a plaque, with all the other poor souls who were transported to their deaths in 1942 and walked us through what was familiar territory for me. The synagogue just up the side street had been demolished, my school had been pulled down, the Jewish cemetery where we used to visit my father's grave had been turned into gardens, the shop on Masaryk Square where I can still see my mother serving a German soldier after the occupation — all of these were no more. But the earlier shop was still there, now used by a travel agent, and the family apartment on the far corner of Bank Strasse (as it used to be) still stood, though the surrounding buildings had been pulled down. Amazingly, we were allowed into the flat by one of the doctors who now has his surgery there and who, having heard a German version of my connection with the premises, took pleasure in showing us all through, thus solving for me a mystery that puzzled me when I was writing an earlier section of this tale: where did my sisters sleep? It had to be a room by the front entrance to the flat, because all the other rooms further along were crystal clear to me, but there was no door that I could recall: how could I not know where my sisters slept? I was really annoyed with myself for my failure of memory, but the answer, when we saw it, explained it all: the one door into my sisters' room was outside on the landing, before the front door was reached, while another door, inside the flat, was reached by going through the parlour, a secret from little boys like me! That said, setting foot again in my bed/living space and looking out of the window at the urban landscape of my childhood gave me a strange feeling of satisfaction. This feeling was further enhanced the next day in Prague, when we were able, by following the instructions that Judita's friend had carefully prepared for us, to visit the National Archive and come away with a copy of Alfred Stiller's birth certificate. The astonishing coincidence of Tom Elliott's visit to Dudley Rotary Club on the evening of my *Desert Island Discs* provided me with rich rewards.

As if that were not enough, the coincidences (or miracles, if you prefer) have continued to fill the months, through 2008 into 2009. Firstly, by getting into conversation with complete strangers in the gallery at the de Montford Hall on the occasion of Jean Humphries being honoured with a Fellowship by Leicester University, we met Professor Felix Beck and his wife: Felix turned out also to be a Czech by birth and hails from Opava, just down the road from Ostrava. Through Felix, I became known to the Ostrava group at Kingston-upon-Thames and thus came to meet David Lawson, who seems to be the focal point for everything relating to Ostrava in this country. Almost immediately after a meeting with David, he informed me that Peter Erben, now 88 years old and living in Ashkelon in Israel, had been trying to contact me for 64 years, since the end of the war.

An exchange of letters with Peter, whose delight at finding me at long last shines through his words, reveals that he met my 18-year-old sister Ilse in 1940/41 when she was on the staff of the Jewish Community Center in Ostrava as a waitress and they fell in love. Through those anxious months leading up to the removal of the Jews from Ostrava in the summer and autumn of 1942, Ilse and Peter were close companions and gave each other hope and support. When my mother and sisters were transported to Teresienstadt (Teresin), the Czech concentration camp, in September of 1942, Peter and his family were also taken. He was there with them a week later when they were moved on to "the East" which, in their case, meant Treblinka, a place from which nobody returned and where nobody survived. Curiously, more than 60 years after these tragic events, my heart is still filled with joy to know that my sisters (because there was some love in Trude's life also with Peter's friend Honza Mayer) met young men whom they could love in their last months alive — and that is something to be grateful for.

Peter's own route to survival I have yet to discover. I wonder now what other coincidences are waiting for me as my 80th year progresses?

Both Margaret and I have been blest with the ability to form the sort of friendships which were not only happy at the time, but proved to endure the passing of the years. To all these friends we owe a lasting debt, for life without friends, like life without children and grandchildren, can be very cold indeed. It is to friends and associates who were willing to go that extra mile in putting forward my name for an honour that I owe the distinction which, deserved or not, was awarded to me in the summer of 2006 by the Prince of Wales at Buckingham Palace. Who would have guessed at that destination for the 10-year-old boy, around whose neck his mother tearfully hung a name card, asking the other occupants of the compartment to keep a friendly eye on Fredi Stiller as she saw him off to Vienna and the unknown

THE STILLER

Aharon Stille

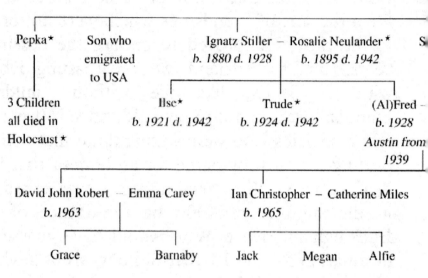

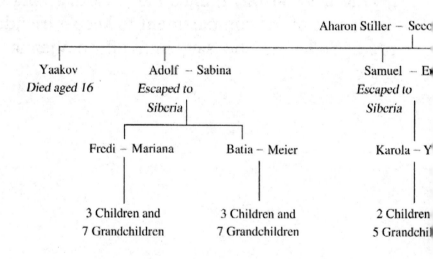

rst Wife

emigrated to USA   Sala★

garet Colam   One son and
.1929   large family
                   in Israel

elen Margaret – Jerome Levé   Rebecca Marie – Nicholas Bolton
    b.1966   *b.1969*

homas   Sebastian   Amelie   Katie   Molly

ife, Cila★

                  Rose★   Bronia★

                 2 Children★   2 Children★
               died in Holocaust died in Holocaust

★ *Died in Holocaust*

Also available in ISIS Large Print:

A Birmingham Backstreet Boyhood

Graham V. Twist

"Mom bought me a second-hand pilot's leather helmet. It was miles too big for me, but I wore it day and night nevertheless. One day running up the street it fell over my eyes and I ran into the corner of a brick and concrete cover that they used to put over the cellar gratings."

Graham Twist's memoir is a fascinating, funny and poignant recollection of growing up in the slums of Nechells and Aston in 1940s Birmingham.

Despite hard living conditions and a distinct lack of money, a strong community spirit prevailed and families and neighbourhoods were close-knit. The womenfolk in particular took great pride in their homes, however humble. In those tough times you hoped nobody noticed you going to the "pop shop" to pawn precious valuables to get enough money to pay the rent or buy food for the family . . .

ISBN 978-0-7531-9580-2 (hb)
ISBN 978-0-7531-9581-9 (pb)

Child From Home

John T. Wright

"Very slowly we began to move and the great black train groaned as it heaved its fully laden carriages out of the station and we were off, blissfully unaware that we were never to see our house or our pet tortoise again."

In 1939, John Wright, a four-year-old boy from a deprived but loving Middlesborough home, was uprooted from his family and evacuated to a large house in North Yorkshire. His story is not unlike any other during the upheaval of wartime, but in this remarkably lucid and detailed set of recollections, he tells his story of love, loss and life with the delight and fear of a wartime child. His poignant memories of cruelty and hurt are set against a voyage of discovery as he explores the Yorkshire countryside, coming of age in a unique environment, only to be struck by unbearable tragedy.

ISBN 978-0-7531-9566-6 (hb)
ISBN 978-0-7531-9567-3 (pb)